Mountain Leadership

Eric Langmuir

The official handbook of the
Mountain Leadership Training Boards
of Great Britain

SCPR

Published by the Scottish Council of Physical Recreation
4 Queensferry St, Edinburgh EH2 4PB *Telephone:* 031-225 5544

Contents

Foreword

This handbook has been produced by the Scottish Mountain Leadership Training Board to help all those who take part in training for Mountain Leadership Certificates, whether as students or teachers. Each year more and more boys and girls from schools and clubs have been given an opportunity to discover the beauty and challenge of mountains, to enrich their experience and, perhaps, to find a lasting interest and recreation. Mountains can be tackled safely only if knowledge and guidance are available and, unfortunately, ignorant or incompetent leadership has been the cause of many accidents in recent years. It is now generally agreed that the responsibility of taking parties of young people on to the mountains is a serious one, requiring at least a minimum standard of training along nationally accepted lines. In Scotland, as in England and Wales, schemes of training have been set up, therefore, leading to certificates recognised by education authorities and youth organisations so that there may be both safety and enjoyment on the hills.

Throughout Britain there are now comprehensive schemes available under the auspices of the Mountain Leadership Training Boards. They include more advanced courses for those intending to become mountaineering instructors but it is at the basic level of mountain leadership that there is a particular demand for guidance

on training. The notes which follow, therefore, have been prepared for this purpose. They include a special section on the Winter Certificate which, in Scotland, is intended for those wishing to take parties out on the mountains under the extremely severe conditions which can arise at almost any time of the year but especially during the long winters. The Scottish Board works in close liaison with its counterpart for England and Wales, the certificates awarded are mutually recognised and the schemes of training as described in these notes are jointly approved by both Boards. There are certain differences in some of the administrative arrangements, including the assessment of candidates, and these are listed in the appendices.

Mountain Leadership training has become a reality through the goodwill, co-operation and voluntary effort of many individuals and organisations. The Board is grateful to the Scottish Council of Physical Recreation, in particular, for sponsoring its activities and for encouraging the publication of this handbook. While the production of the handbook has been the responsibility of the whole Board, the Board is indebted to Eric Langmuir who has been not only the editor but, in essence, the author also of these notes.

JOHN W. COOK, *Chairman,*
Scottish Mountain Leadership Training Board

Author's Note

These notes have been compiled to assist Candidates for the Summer and Winter Mountain Leadership Certificates. It was never intended that they should compete with the many excellent books which already exist on the subject of mountaineering, but rather that they should supplement these works drawing attention to new material where appropriate and summarising the special requirements of the Certificate. For this reason certain chapters have been treated more fully than others especially those which deal with subjects not covered by existing publications; for example exposure and its relevance to expedition planning, snow structure and the development of

avalanche hazard and so on. Other topics such as rock climbing and snow and ice climbing which have been exhaustively covered elsewhere are regarded more from the point of view of the instructor and the arrangement of subject matter than from any technical standpoint. This inevitably has led to a certain lack of continuity for which I must take full responsibility.

Finally I should like to record my thanks to those members of the Board who have made individual contributions to the booklet and in particular to Ralph Blain, Murray Scott and Hamish Brown, and to the staff at Glenmore Lodge.

ERIC LANGMUIR

Introduction

The element of risk is a fundamental theme running through all outdoor activities. In fact it is their mainspring. It is present even in the most controlled of conditions. It is present in the imagination of the novice rock climber – 'Will the rope really hold me if I fall?' Of course it will, but the doubt and fear are there and must be overcome. It is present too in the unexpected, in the objective dangers of our sport; the hold that weakens; the rock that falls; the lightning that strikes; and through the actions and mistakes of others. To avoid these multitudinous hazards we would do well to stay in our beds.

How then can we preserve some sort of balance between the adventurous element of outdoor activities on the one hand and the safety element on the other? At first sight the two appear to be incompatible and yet how often one finds that the top performer in a particular field is also the safest.

The answer seems to lie in the right sort of combination of training and experience. It matters not whether the training is given by more experienced friends or by an instructor at a mountain centre. The vital thing is that it should be based on the accepted code of technique and safety. Far from detracting from enjoyment, observance of this code broadens the safety margin and enables more ambitious projects to be enjoyed in safety. There is no such thing as a fully trained mountaineer and it would be a bold man and a foolish one who claimed that he had nothing more to learn.

Experience is the tough school of graduate training where the techniques learned in the shadow of a leader can be put to the test. This experience should, as far as possible, be matched to the appropriate stage of training achieved. It would be foolhardy in the extreme for example to attempt to lead a difficult ice climb on the basis of a knowledge of summer rock climbing in the Lake District. No amount of training or attendance at courses can compensate for a lack of this practical and individual experience. No amount of climbing as second on the rope is going to produce a good leader. Certainly, it will produce a good second or a good 'party' man, but the decisions that count are made in the van and the potential leader must find his own feet here, without the comforting knowledge that he has a long-stop, should things go wrong. A decision without the pressure of consequence is hardly a decision at all. The Mountain Leadership Training Board recognises this and insists that all candidates gain a minimum of genuine leading experience before coming for their final course of Assessment.

To say that in this way we can achieve a balance between 'challenge' and 'safety' is wishful thinking. The best we can hope for is an uneasy truce. It is foolish to expect a youngster to equate these two sensibly and it is in this department that he needs most guidance. It is hoped that the Mountain Leadership Certificate will make this informed guidance more readily available to the ever increasing number of young people going into the hills.

The Summer Certificate

1 Navigation

Good navigation is the fundamental theme of the Mountain Leadership Certificate, and thorough familiarity with the subject is expected at Assessment. Far too many accidents can be traced to an original error in route finding. It is not enough just to be able to follow a set course in fine weather at a low level. Absolute certainty in blind navigation in the most severe weather conditions is required and experience of these conditions is an essential part of training whether it is obtained at the course or at some other time and place.

The assessment itself will be based on the points listed in the Syllabus (see Appendix B) and will take place throughout the week, from written and oral examination to practical navigation on each day's journey and on the final expedition. The maps used will normally be from the 1″ or 2½″ O.S. Series and candidates are expected to use a Silva or similar type of compass. Heavy prismatics and '3d. bit' compasses are equally unacceptable.

No person is entirely safe in the mountains if he cannot use map and compass no matter how knowledgeable and experienced the leader. For reasons outside his control the members of the party can become separated and therefore it is important that each individual should be given sufficient basic instruction to enable him to find his way to safety. In the field of navigation then the party leader must be able to give such basic instruction. Training is arranged with this in mind and hints are given on methods of instruction and teaching aids.

The lesson plan which follows does not set out to explain map and compass work but rather to act as a guide to both the student and to the potential instructor as to what should be covered and how. One thing is certain and that is that if properly put across it can be a fascinating and rewarding subject.

Lesson plan

Introduction

Topic	Content	Aids to Instruction
HISTORY OF NAVIGATION	Natural navigation of the ancient peoples of the world (e.g. Polynesians) and in primitive societies today. Stress 'home on base' reference system and paramount importance of OBSERVATION – No Sixth Sense! Map and Compass does not dispense with need for observation.	To stress need for training and discipline, blindfold and ask to walk to fixed point.
EARLY PICTORIAL MAPS	Describe some of the great exploratory journeys and show the maps resulting from them. Point out differences in methods of presentation.	Many fascinating old maps are now available as prints.
MODERN SURVEY METHODS	History of the Ordnance Survey. Triangulation to aerial photography.	For interest only.

The Map

Topic	Content	Aids to Instruction
THE MODERN MAP	Firmly establish meaning of map as plan or aerial view. Align photo, model and map to establish relationship between them.	Air photograph, relief model and map of the same area and on the same scale.
SCALE	Necessity for and selection of suitable scales for different purposes (e.g. motoring, cycling, walking, building). The representative fraction and continental scales (2½″ map equivalent to 1/25,000).	A series of maps of varying scales showing some easily recognisable feature, such as a loch, each with the area of the largest scale map marked in outline.
MAP REFERENCES	The grid system, national and international.	Best explained on a blackboard at first. Plenty of practice later both ways, map to reference and vice versa.
CONVENTIONAL SIGNS	A shorthand system. Illustrate different methods of representation (pictorial, initials, colour etc.).	Various guessing games can be devised to stimulate interest. 'MAPPO', using map symbols instead of numbers, as in Bingo, is a useful game.
PLACE NAMES	Compare the common ones from Scotland, England, Wales and Ireland.	Always try to create an interest in the meaning of the Gaelic place names.

A practical session at this point, before the introduction of contours, breaks up the theoretical instruction and helps to consolidate what has been learned. Courses should be short and simple, following roads and tracks and students should be accompanied, at least initially, so that their problems can be sorted out before they lose the thread.

Contours

Topic	Content	Aids to Instruction
CONTOUR LINES	Trace the history of the representation of relief on old maps. Firmly establish the principle of contour lines and the vertical interval between them. This is a crucial point in the understanding of maps. Use every aid at your disposal.	Plumpudding maps, hachuring, colouring etc. Show examples. ■ Stone in trough. Add water inch by inch and mark water line on stone. ■ Slice up half a turnip or potato. ■ Use a stack of glass trays, each with a single contour line drawn on it superimposed on the original map. ■ A relief model before plastering showing stepped structure. ■ Sand tray work.
	Gradients, convex and concave slope, spurs, valleys and other topographical features.	Illustrate with examples from prepared map and also by use of models as above.

A practical session should follow bringing in various aspects of relief. The terrain must be suitably chosen so that the differences of relief are sufficiently clear on the map.

The Compass

Topic	Content	Aids to Instruction
ORIGINS	The magic needle of the Chinese. Where it points and why. Eight points of the compass – degrees – angles (Bearings).	Charts and blackboard.
NORTH POINTS	Magnetic and Grid or True North.	At the elementary stage do not confuse the issue by distinguishing between Grid North and True North. Use a world globe.
THE COMPASS	The Silva Compass and its component parts. Explanation of its use as:	Large plastic model available from B. J. Ward.
	■ a protractor, e.g. measuring angles (bearings) on the map.	Warn of effect of metal objects such as cameras, ice axes, etc.
	■ a compass, e.g. (i) Setting the map; (ii) Taking a bearing out of doors on a feature and the identification of this on the map. This involves the conversion of a magnetic to a true bearing and the use of the compass again as a protractor.	Plenty of examples until familiar.
	As in (i) measuring a bearing on the map, converting it to a magnetic bearing and setting this on the compass.	More examples. Insist on a rough visual check of the angle from the map.
WALKING ON A BEARING	Matching-up needle and walking on bearing set. Hints for use in bad conditions.	Practise exhaustively later.
TIME AND DISTANCE	Speed in relation to terrain and other factors. Naismith's rule as a rough guide (3 m.p.h. $+ \frac{1}{2}$ hour per 1000 ft. climbing).	
ROUTE SELECTION	Choice of best route. Essential bearings, escape routes, etc. Route card with estimated times.	Fill in sample route cards for various expeditions.
ON THE MARCH	Compensation for detours. Encourage use of natural advantages of terrain and deliberate 'AIM-OFF' to hit target. Error alertness and early correction. Safety precautions and methods in bad visibility.	
RESECTION	Establish location with back bearings from visible features.	

Much of this instruction is best done out of doors. If at all possible each phase of theoretical instruction should be immediately followed by practical work to implant it firmly in the mind of the student.

Simple navigation courses can be great fun if intelligently laid out. They should if possible encircle the base so that a bad mistake can always be rectified by a quick return for further instructions. The course should not be too long and should become progressively more difficult towards the finish. In safe country students should travel singly or in pairs. In larger groups all the calculations tend to be done by the brightest ones. Problems of all kinds may be set en route including identification of features, sketch notes, collection of rock or plant specimens and so on; anything in fact which will stimulate the student to practice the skills previously learned indoors. The sport of Orienteering and simple map-making by compass traverse are other excellent ways of encouraging an interest in Navigation.

Finally it is well to remember that this skill is really only put to the test in a situation of stress and anxiety when perhaps conditions have deteriorated to such an extent that visibility is reduced almost to nil. It is under this sort of pressure that you cannot afford to make a mistake.

2 Hillwalking

Number in party

Without a doubt this is the most important and yet the most neglected of all the factors concerned with mountain safety. Perhaps this is because it can never be formulated as an unvarying rule. There are too many other factors which have a bearing on the number of people who can safely be taken on a mountain walk: the length of the route, the type of ground surface and special difficulties of the terrain such as rock ridges and so on, the conditions to be expected overhead and underfoot for example wind, rain and snow and the fitness, age and sex of the members of the party. Not only are large parties of 15, 20 and sometimes even 30 highly dangerous on the hill, but they stifle interest and make good instruction impossible. One person cannot possibly look after such large groups even in the easiest of terrain and when things go wrong troubles tend to multiply in proportion to the number of people in the party.

As a general rule hillwalking groups should number between three and ten, the ideal being about six; the sort of number the leader can be aware of without actually counting heads. If the route is a long one or perhaps one which involves some scrambling or ridge walking, six should be taken as the maximum. NEVER go alone. Three is taken to be the minimum safe number since in the event of an accident one member of the party can stay with the injured person while the other goes to summon help. This minimum becomes the maximum if long sections of difficult ground are to be encountered; the sort of ground which necessitates the use of a safety rope and demands of the leader a basic knowledge of rock climbing and rope handling.

Equipment and clothing

The equipment carried by each member of the party must be checked by the leader before leaving base. A full list of equipment is given in Appendix E.

■ Each member of the group should have:
Map / compass / whistle / rucksack / large polythene bag / personal first aid kit / lunch / emergency ration, and in winter: Ice axe / torch / goggles in addition to the clothing and spare items mentioned below.

■ The party leader should have in addition:
120 feet of No. 2 Rope / a comprehensive first aid kit / duvet jacket or sleeping bag / mini flare pack or red flare.

As with personal equipment, clothing must be checked before departure. Boots should be comfortable and allow for one pair of thick stockings. Blisters must be treated immediately and not allowed to develop into deep sores. Woollen underwear is recommended for winter wear though string vests are popular as the wide mesh retains body heat and helps to prevent the top clothing becoming wet with perspiration.

Breeches or trousers, but not jeans, should be worn. Remember that several thin sweaters afford greater warmth and flexibility than one thick one. For all high level walking a waterproof anorak or cagoule is essential. Intelligent use of clothing can greatly increase the comfort of the walk. Don't let your party labour uphill wearing all their clothing. If practicable insist that they remove the outer layers and put them on again during rest periods. Spare clothing, including sweater, gloves, stockings, and over-trousers should be wrapped in a polythene bag and carried in the communal sack. A balaclava helmet and gloves should be taken on all expeditions when cold conditions are likely to be encountered.

Method

■ On roads or flat ground journeys are usually measured by miles, but on the hills it is more expedient to measure in hours. A rough guide when estimating the time of a walk for an average lightly equipped party is to allow one hour for every three miles plus half an hour for each thousand feet of climbing.

Route cards giving estimated times of arrival at various points, together with compass bearings, are invaluable in poor conditions. Escape routes should be noted and a bad weather alternative entered on the card. The simplest type of route card takes the following form:

From	*To*	*Distance*
Height	*Estimated Time*	*Compass Bearing*

■ Speed is of less importance than economy of effort. To hurry, except in extenuating circumstances, is foolish.

'Tail end Charlies' must be encouraged and not left to struggle on their own to become exhausted and depressed. Keep together and on no account send any member of the party back on his own. Except in dire emergency the party should act as a single unit.

■ Rhythm is essential to good hill walking: jerky movements, springing and flexing the knees by taking too high a step tire the muscles and should be avoided. The leg should be allowed to swing forward like a pendulum; the natural swing of the body assists this movement. There should be no conscious use of the leg muscles. To assist rhythm and balance the hands should be kept free at all times. Spare clothes, etc., should be carried in the rucksack or tied round the waist.

To maintain rhythm, the same speed of pace should be used on all types of ground, the length of the pace being shortened for steep or difficult ground and lengthened for easy ground.

■ The feet should be placed down flat with a deliberate step, resting the heels on any available projections such as stones or tufts of grass. Where the slope is very steep, zig-zagging will assist the walker. Good rhythm and setting the feet is the sign of the experienced hill walker.

■ When descending, overstriding and putting the foot down heavily should be avoided as these jar the body and therefore fatigue the walker. A controlled descent can be assisted by placing the toes against projections. Running downhill, though good fun, can be tiring. A good walker uses downhill periods to rest the muscles.

Scree running is also fun, but it is bad for boots and unless closely supervised can be dangerous. If you have to negotiate a scree make absolutely sure that your party is deployed in such a way that stones dislodged by one do not fall onto another.

■ Constant stopping and starting breaks up walking rhythm and should be avoided. Halts should only be made at fixed intervals based on time and ground; these halts should be of a short duration, on average 5 – 10 minutes every hour. Large meals should be avoided – 'a little and often' being the better approach to eating during a day on the hills. It is a good plan to retain a portion of the day's food until all difficult ground has been crossed and so maintain a reserve of food in case the unforeseen should occur.

Most streams in the mountains are fit to drink from. The body needs to replace fluid lost in sweat, in breathing, etc., and contrary to popular belief drinking is to be encouraged – 'little and often' once again being the safest maxim.

■ Constant vigilance should be exercised, as weather conditions can deteriorate with extreme rapidity in hill country. Check the weather forecast before leaving.

Changes of weather can produce serious problems for a walker, and great care should be taken that one does not over-reach one's ability. Most accidents due to weather occur through rashness. Act before the weather dictates its own terms.

■ Exposure is an ever present danger with young people in the mountains and all leaders must be familiar with its recognition and treatment. If your party is fit, dry, well fed and watered and in good spirit you have little to fear. If they are not, then you must modify your route to suit their condition and capabilities.

'It is the additional factor of physical exhaustion over and above cold which kills quickly. Death has overtaken whole parties who, thinking they must keep moving at all costs, have bashed on, instead of resting in some shelter before exhaustion supervened.' *Dr. Duff.*

■ No attempt must be made to cross mountain streams in spate where there is possible danger to life unless each member of the party can be adequately safeguarded. Youngsters should not be given routes to follow independently which might involve the crossing of such streams.

■ Severe electrical storms are unusual in British mountains. In the event of one, do not seek shelter under overhangs or in cracks in the cliff face or against large prominent boulders. Avoid being the prominent object in the neighbourhood. Get off peaks and ridges and sit it out on open coarse-blocked scree. There is no need to throw away your axe, camera or other ironmongery – you may need them later and they do not 'attract' lightning any more than you do yourself.

■ Rope the party together when visibility is very poor and when there is the likelihood that a slip might develop into a dangerous slide. Remember too that a small error in navigation can lead you to the edge of a cliff.

■ In addition to its chilling effect the wind can exert sufficient force to sweep a party off its feet. Be particularly careful round the tops of coires or on exposed ridges where a fall could be disastrous.

Good technique and safety measures can be learned. Good leadership and instruction is an art which embraces much more than mere technical skill. Your job as the leader of a party is to stimulate interest and safe enjoyment in everything which the mountains have to offer.

3 Camping and Expeditions

These notes deal with a vital part of the certificate work as much of young people's outdoor activity is based on camping and expeditions, which are influenced themselves by other factors (i.e. strength of party, weather). Misadventure could have serious consequences and candidates are urged to attain as much experience as possible.

Camping is the ability to live as comfortably as possible under any weather conditions in remote areas with the minimum of equipment needed to ensure adequate shelter, feeding, and expedition activity.

Leaders should constantly be teaching by example. Comfort, safety and enjoyment lie in a thousand little knacks, too numerous to list. These notes indicate some of the more important points. Many aspects of camping and expedition activity can be rehearsed beforehand, and this is essential, both for personal assurance and the safety of young people who cannot be watched all the time. The year of experience between Basic Training and Assessment is the time to acquire camping and expedition skills and routine.

The Party should be reasonably fit before starting. Care should be taken not to overburden. Check for anyone with disabilities or special medical requirements. Ensure parents signed approval to partake at their responsibility. Check insurance. If travelling, use 'Kwells'.

The Timetable should be flexible and there should be some progression from easy to more difficult undertakings. If the weather is severe, stay put if possible; certainly not moving merely to stick to an armchair plan. Mountain weather is unpredictable. Allow for this when planning. Do not attempt too long marches. Very hot weather can also be exhausting: if necessary be up at five and finish the day's walk by noon. Use local knowledge as well as maps, guides, etc.

Daily Routine An early start always pays off. Work out a system that can be used by the party each day. Everyone should be employed. From waking to departure should not be longer than two hours for an efficient team. Try to be settled in a new site before evening. Tents should, as far as possible, operate as independent units, though, if weather is set fair, it may be quicker for each tent to deal with one part of a meal. Two tents, pitched door to door, can also operate as a unit. Do not hesitate to stop for a 'brew-up' or a swim during the day. They are valuable mentally and physically. Check at the end of a trip to see what was carried and never used – question whether to take it again. Ensure that people wash adequately and change clothes before sleeping.

Food Adequate (some 4000+ calories per day) and appetising feeding is a vital part of any well run expedition. See to it that your party takes a hot breakfast and evening meal each day. A communal brew of hot, sweet tea immediately on arrival at the camp site is an excellent morale booster and paves the way to a good meal. Lightweight expeditions can make use of the wide range of dehydrated foods now available on the market. Be careful to select those which have a reasonably short cooking time and which can be cooked in a single pot. Dehydrated foods are of course expensive, but allow a great saving in weight and therefore of energy.

Personal Clothing A comprehensive list of recommended clothing and equipment is given in Appendix 'E'.

■ Never assume that the members of your party are properly kitted out. Before leaving inspect all equipment and personal clothing.

■ Insist on warm trousers or breeches and adequate head cover.

■ A waterproof outer is essential whether it be the specially designed cagoule or an ex W.D. gas cape. If of the latter type make sure that there is some means of tying it to the body in windy conditions.

■ All spare clothing must be carried in a polythene bag. Try to achieve a sensible balance between adequate protection and the extra weight to be carried.

■ A dry set of clothes should always be kept for night wear or emergency. Wet clothes can often be dried out over night and in any case it is normally better to put on damp clothes in the morning than risk wetting your dry change.

Boots and Care of Feet Boots are essential for comfort, safety and efficiency. Make sure they are broken in before an expedition and that they are kept clean and well maintained by replacement of the natural oils in the leather as necessary. They should offer good ankle support, they should protect the sole of the foot from sharp stones and they should be fairly rigid across the sole. Some flexibility in a forward direction makes for more comfortable walking and a bellows-type tongue helps to keep out the water. The limitations of the vibram or moulded rubber sole should be clearly understood. They are slippery on hard snow or ice, on vegetation of any kind and on wet, greasy rock.

The condition of your feet can make or mar an expedition. Keep them in good order and insist that your charges do the same: wash regularly / use clean, well fitting stockings or socks, a single pair of loop stitched stockings is best or two pairs of wool ones / toe nails should be cut straight and kept short / regular applications of surgical spirit harden the feet / the slightest irritation should be plastered at once. Blisters are uncomfortable and a hindrance and potential danger to the whole party. They should be pricked with a sterilised needle to allow the liquid to escape and then plastered. Change the plaster daily and allow every opportunity for the area to harden up in the fresh air.

Load Packing and Carrying

TYPES

■ The framed sack of the 'Commando' style is quite unsuitable since it forces the wearer into a crouched position. However, better designs are available which are relatively light in weight, which distribute the load well and which allow ventilation of the back.

■ The pack frame can be adapted to carry a variety of loads and is generally accepted as being the most efficient method of carrying a heavy load.

■ The unframed sack is light and comfortable to carry and can be used as a mattress or to provide protection for the feet at night. There is no ventilation for the back and the weight tends to be rather more unevenly distributed.

PACKING

■ Articles needed during the journey or immediately on reaching the camp site should be on top or in side pockets, i.e. food for the day, first aid kit, tent and so on. / Do not have articles dangling from the outside of the sack. / Heavy articles should be kept as high as possible. / Balance the weight and avoid sharp edges and corners against the back. / Stove and fuel should be kept in a well sealed polythene bag and stored in a side pocket or well away from food. / Adjust shoulder and waist straps as necessary.

WEIGHT

■ Your total load should never exceed one-third of the body weight and for young people 35 lbs. should be the absolute maximum.

CARRYING

■ As far as possible the load should be kept high on the back and in such a position that the weight acts vertically downwards through the spine. This principle has been used successfully for centuries by all the primitive people of the world.

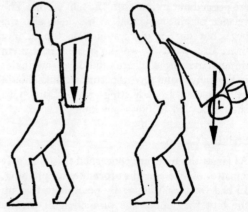

Fig. 1: This   Not This

Tents

Poor quality tents should not be used in mountains. For the wet and windy conditions so common in the U.K. it is advisable to have a sewn-in ground sheet, down to earth all-round fly sheet and strong alloy 'A' poles front and rear. Many so called 'mountain tents' are in fact designed for high altitude work abroad in conditions of extreme dry-cold and are quite unsuited to our normal weather. Each tent should be a self-contained unit with its own stove, dixies, food, etc., sufficient for the occupants.

Siting the Camp

A good site should provide shelter from the prevailing wind. The ground should be as flat as possible and relatively free from lumps, tussocks and boulders. It should be well drained and safe from potential flooding. A handy water supply is almost essential though don't pitch too near a noisy mountain stream if you want an undisturbed night's rest. Trees may provide some protection from the wind but don't pitch directly underneath them; although they offer some immediate shelter from the rain eventually large drops form and these are much more effective in penetrating the fly sheet.

Tent Pitching

Even if the weather seems set fair allow for the worst when pitching your tent. Put the back end into the wind and peg out the groundsheet first to ensure tent shaping. Erect the windward end first and peg out all main guys. Other guys are pegged out in line with the tent seams. The valance may be weighted with stones, also the pegs, but do not place stones on top of guy lines. In a wind the sawing actions fray them through in no time. There should be no wrinkles in the canvas and any unnatural strains should be corrected by adjusting guys. Door tabs should be tied in bows not knots.

Striking Camp

As far as the tents are concerned this is largely a matter of reversing the procedure for pitching. In bad weather it is usually possible to fold up the tent first under the protection of the fly sheet. All pegs should be cleaned and all the parts stowed away in their bags. On returning to base, tents should be hung to dry out thoroughly and examined carefully for any damage before storing. Check the site before leaving to see nothing is forgotten and no litter is left. After a few days it should be hard to tell that the site has been used.

Bedding – Warmth and Comfort

■ A sleeping bag is far lighter and warmer than blankets. It is worth buying a good quality down bag as it will last a long time with care. It should be kept dry and clean and stored unrolled.

■ Much cold comes from below and insulation is recommended. A sewn-in groundsheet helps. A layer or two of newspapers, tarred paper or frameless rucksack is useful. An air bed or foam mattress gives comfort as well as insulation.

■ In winter a second sleeping bag may be needed. Always do something about cold, if necessary light a stove or exercise, don't just lie!

■ It is often possible to pack the underside of the groundsheet with bracken, heather or grass to improve comfort and insulation.

■ It is more comfortable to sleep head uphill if on a slope.

■ Polythene bags are useful for storing: unwanted clothes (useful as pillow) / wet clothes if inside at all / personal belongings / sugar, salt, potato powder or anything else in breakable packets / emergency bags for travel sickness.

■ Boots should not be worn inside tents. Wet clothes should be taken off before entry if possible. If soaked to the skin, remove all clothing, get into sleeping bag and prepare hot, sweet drinks.

■ Store tins, wet clothes, ropes, anything sheep, cows, dogs will not eat, under the flysheets. Pans, stoves, water carriers should be easily within reach.

■ Tents without flysheets will leak if the canvas is rubbed. The obvious solution is a flysheet, otherwise movement has to be restricted. A small sponge is useful to mop up leak spots or spilt tea, etc.

■ Newspapers are useful in camping: for insulation under bedding / for cleaning material / to keep under supplies, cutlery or pans to prevent dirt or grease spreading / under a pullover for body insulation / helping to dry boots / helping to start fires.

■ The following are some useful items: Torch (remove battery to avoid accidental switch-on in travel); compass (Silva type are the 'best buy'); whistle (a pea whistle is better than a policeman's); maps (1″ O.S. are best); plastic paraffin jars; tin opener (small ones, costing 6d., can fold into a wallet); brillo pads; toilet paper; knife; spare bootlaces (for any purpose); first aid kit; a 120 ft. nylon No. 2 rope; emergency rations in a special box; cutlery; deep plate and mug (not china); plimsolls (wear on bare feet if wet, avoiding wet socks); a band saw can cut firewood easily; a small size fish slice is valuable; as is an egg whisk for mixing milk powder;

sewing kit; shoe kit; writing materials; transistor (for weather forecasts); anti-midge cream and / or spray (May to October); alarm clock (folding); camera; small binoculars.

Hygiene

■ Water should be collected above the site and washing should be done below.

■ Nails should be clean and washing of hands insisted on after using lavatories or before handling food.

■ If at all possible take your rubbish home with you especially if the site is accessible and likely to be used frequently. Otherwise rubbish should be burnt and buried in a deep pit. Tins should be opened at both ends, flattened and burnt.

■ Glass is unnecessary in the first place (use plastic bags or containers or light tins and transfer jar contents into these) but on no account must be smashed. Take empties home! Livestock damage is caused by tins and glass carelessly disposed. Polythene bags are particularly lethal to animals.

■ Toilet facilities depend on length of stay. Where at all permanent, a latrine trench is advisable. Excrement must be buried at least 6″ below surface. There should be no trace left.

Stoves

TYPES

■ Camping Gaz: This is clean, requires no priming, but is expensive and, for half an hour before a cartridge runs out, burns at an infuriatingly low pressure.

■ Pressure stove: These require priming with solid 'Meta' fuel or meths, but give a wide variety of pressure.They are very cheap to run. Petrol stoves are not recommended for inexperienced young people.

SAFETY FACTORS

■ Changing Gaz cartridges or filling stoves should be done in the open and away from candles or any naked light.

■ Experience in using stoves must be had before going off on expeditions when their lighting and use may be within tents or shelter.

■ Paraffin pressure stoves in fact burn paraffin vapour and pumping too soon will result in flooding. This causes dangerous flaring and soot is deposited which will ultimately choke the nipple. Pricking (only when needed) to clear stoves, as well as priming, should be done outside, if possible.

■ Make sure you have the correct fuel. Because of this danger, parties of young people are advised to use paraffin stoves only. Petrol stoves always have additional risks.

■ Do not overfill a stove. When doing anything to a stove, always remove pans. When stirring pans, always hold on to the handle. Scalding accidents are common. Make sure handles are up or extended properly so that they do not hang down near the flame to become dangerously hot.

■ Patience is the most important point in stove control.

Fire in Tents

The main causes are: mis-use of stoves / cigarettes / candle or lighting.

PRECAUTIONS

See above, but also, do not fall asleep smoking or with a candle or stove left burning. (Elementary – but it happens constantly!) Long candles should be snapped in half to make them less unstable. Even placing them up on a tin usually ensures that if they topple they land end on and so extinguish the flame. Some safety holder is easily created. With other forms of lighting – wick or pressure lamps, etc., care must be taken to ensure adequate ventilation.

A small internal fire can quickly be smothered with a sleeping bag, with little damage to the bag but, if the roof or walls go up, it is vital to get out fast. Poles and, if necessary, main guys, should be collapsed to smother the fire. Any other method is ineffective as it is too slow. Exterior poles are useful for this. A stove giving real trouble should be thrown outside at once. Work stoves near the entrance – if you must have them inside at all.

Outdoor fires may be pleasant but great care must be taken to ensure no fire risk to tents and to forests or dry hillsides from falling hot sparks. Turf must be removed and replaced over the dead ashes. On no account should a smouldering fire be left. Rubbish can be burnt sometimes on the rocks of a river bed.

Failure of preparation and ineffective leadership in camping and expeditions can lead to: failure of achievement / dangerous situations or accidents / discomfort / discouragement.

4 Rock climbing and rope management

The rock climbing section of both Mountain Leadership Training Boards is entitled 'Basic Rock Climbing Skills' and this title is defined as follows: 'the small amount of rock climbing training included in the course is not intended to train leaders as rock climbers. Its purpose is to familiarise the candidates with *elementary* techniques, to enable them to appreciate the limits of what should be attempted by a party without rock-climbing experience, to recognise difficulties and potentially dangerous terrain and to give competent help in cases of emergency.

This definition should be read carefully by candidates, instructors and assessors. As an aid to the understanding of the needs, the major assessment points will be dealt with first.

Assessment ("Rock climbing")

The object of assessment is to discover whether or not the candidate is confident and familiar with the rope and that he can achieve speed of action in getting it into use.

He must: be able to lead on easy rock in descent as well as ascent; be able to abseil; be able to find and use suitable anchors, *quickly*; be able to hold a falling second; be able to set up the rope as a fixed rope; know the standard calls and signals used for communication; be able to pass on simple instruction in all of these things; be able to select a safe line up a rocky hillside.

The importance of the inclusion of this small amount of rock-climbing in the syllabus, as a means of understanding the proper use of a safety rope cannot be over-stressed. A rope is a vital piece of equipment for a mountain leader.

Candidates must be aware of this emphasis and of the large gap that exists in their safe supervision of a party in the mountains, if they are not confident in their ability to cope with a situation requiring the use of a safety line. There is no attempt to make them rock climbers in the normally accepted definition of the word.

It is worth remembering that there are many situations apart from graded rock climbs, when the rope is at least desirable and sometimes essential, e.g.:

■ A particularly nervous person, in an intimidating situation, may welcome a safety line.
■ A person suffering from a minor injury (sprained ankle) may need the security of a rope.
■ Used as a handline (wrist loops).
■ Crossing a gully, checking a line of descent, moving across frozen grass (spring or autumn hazard).
■ Going to someone's assistance.
■ Moving together in poor visibility and bad weather. Particularly important on snow covered ground in white-out conditions (even on flat plateau if ringed by crags).

Leaders should always appreciate the technical difficulties as they appear to the novice and be sympathetic towards their mental condition under stress. Psychological and physical succour brought about by the timely and proper use of the rope can make the difference between a serious situation and safe leadership.

Any mountain leader ought to be in a position to advise young people in his care on all aspects of mountain safety including differentiating between rough ground, scrambling, rock-climbing and also steep ground which could normally be walked over but will on occasion need to be avoided or a rope used to safeguard the party.

Mountaineers with considerable rock climbing experience may use, under assessment, any acceptable and safe rope technique, e.g. the methods known as 'Classic' and 'Tarbuck'.

Instruction

To teach the rudiments of the skills of rope handling, to give satisfactory guidance in the selection of sound belays, to make the candidate confident as an 'abseiler' and to allow him an opportunity to lead, means that a full day's instruction is necessary. Whilst a whole day may seem a lot of time, it can be broken up; knots and communications can be done as a separate, indoor session. As far as possible rock-climbing instruction should be conducted at the rock face.

Initially, only No. 4 nylon rope should be used; no slings, karabiners or hemp waist loops. The instruction should be done with the equipment that is normally carried (one rope). As most equipment lists suggest that the safety line can be 100 ft. to 120 ft. of No. 2 nylon, experience of handling and holding should be done with this size of rope as well. It is also desirable that a single, standard knot system be used for tying on.

As a standard approach is considered desirable and to emphasise the need for planned instruction, a lesson plan is given below. Progress will depend on the students themselves and the staff available, but all the topics listed must be covered in basic training.

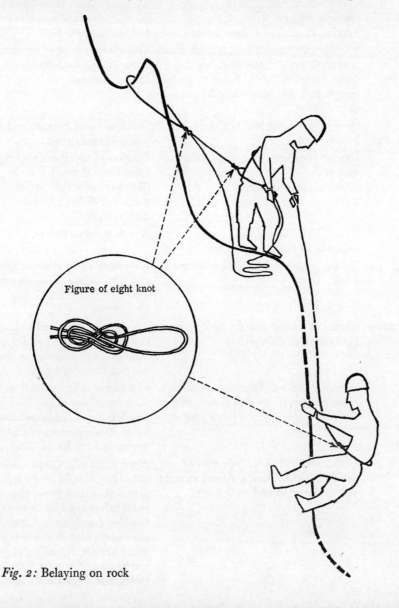

Figure of eight knot

Fig. 2: Belaying on rock

Rock climbing lesson plan

Topic	Content	Notes
EQUIPMENT	Strength of ropes – length – properties of nylon rope – different handling properties of No. 4 and No. 2.	No. 4 and No. 2 ropes – Indoor Session.
ROPE	Coiling, carrying, hanging, storage	Indoor Session.
KNOTS	Figure of eight – overhand.	Indoor Session.
BELAYS	Spike belays. Selection of suitable anchors. Stance. Belay in relation to stance. Thread belay.	No slings used. Emphasise anchor selection – would you abseil from it? Indoor Session.
CALLS	'TAKING IN', 'THAT'S ME', 'CLIMB WHEN YOU'RE READY', 'CLIMBING', 'OK'. Loud and clear use of these terms by everyone. Later 'MORE ROPE', 'TAKE IN'.	Stress importance of communications – vital to standardise. Indoor Session.
SCRAMBLING WITHOUT ROPES	Over broken rock and boulders before reaching crag.	Observation of balance and movement. Warming up.
LOOSE ROCK AND SCREE	Care in handling. Warning shout 'Below'.	Position of members of party on loose scree slope.
CLIMBS	Climbing UP and DOWN.	Simple climbs only at first – perhaps one more difficult to aid differentiation.
MOVEMENT	Use of feet – three-point contact – selection of holds – soundness of rock.	Avoid complex moves.
FALLS	Falling (as second only). Holding a a fall.	Instructor to be close at hand – check all belays. Give warnings. *This is a Controlled Trial.* Use gloves.
ROUTE SELECTION	Choice of easiest line up rock buttress. Estimation of difficulties.	This can be practised at least in theory throughout the day and on neighbouring hillsides as well as on the practice crag itself.
LEADING	Speed or lack of. Selection of holds, route and belay. UP and DOWN. Short pitches – probably one pitch routes.	Climbs must be selected well within the capabilities of the student. Implication of diagonal movement. Stress consequences of bad leader decisions as to route, belays, etc.
ABSEILING	Classic method only. Selection of suitable anchor points. Abseil straight and to the right and to the left.	Always use safety rope under training. They should do enough of this to feel that they could abseil without a safety rope in an emergency. On No. 4 and No. 2 ropes. Don't use belay point as abseil point. Short abseils. Abseiling may be introduced whenever time and instructional staff will allow.

FIXED LINE AND HAND LINES	Use by a party.	Limitations – dangers of.
LEADING THROUGH	Practice, speed of selection and use of belays. Rope handling.	This is most likely how candidates will be assessed – Leading through on the simplest of ground, e.g. a rocky ridge.

Further Training and difference between S.M.L.T.B. & M.L.T.B. Syllabuses

The techniques advocated for basic M.L. training are not necessarily those which would be taught to rock climbers, particularly since no special equipment is used other than the rope. However, the possibility of progression should always be borne in mind by the instructor and interested candidates may be taken a stage further.

The Scottish Board considers the figure of 8 on the bight using a waist belay to be the most satisfactory method of belaying for the non-climbing mountaineer to use while recognising its limitations from a climbing point of view. The English Board goes a stage further and advocates that the 'Classic' belay system be taught where the rope returns to the waist from the belay point and is secured there by a figure of 8 knot, while the active rope is taken under and over the shoulders in the normal way.

Conclusion

The effectiveness of this instruction depends on:
■ Candidates understanding *WHY* all this is being done.
■ An adequate number of competent instructors who also understand the place of this subject in the syllabus, and its treatment. The number of instructors ought to be in the ratio of 1:4 under instruction and 1:2 under assessment.
■ The selection of a suitable piece of rocky terrain to illustrate all the main points mentioned.

During the course instructors will teach the elements of party management in emergencies requiring the use of a rope, explaining who carries the rope and where, describing the ground on which a party might require more than one rope, and emphasising to leaders that their charges must know how to use a rope before they go on the hill. It is far too late to begin instruction in rope handling after a man is in need of it. This argues that the leader must be able to give simple instruction to his party. His ability to do this will be assessed.

5 River Crossing

Preparation

The aim of the training is twofold
■ To acquaint climbers with the dangers of streams in flood.
■ To suggest safe methods of crossing streams which are fordable.

Few climbers or walkers have any idea of the forces involved in moving water. 'I had no idea it was so powerful' is an often heard remark during training sessions on the river. It is one of the prime objects of training to provide this experience under controlled and supervised conditions. It has been said that it is impossible to control conditions and that for this reason river crossing should not be taught to mountain leaders. Burns and rivers are as much part of the mountain environment as rocks and learning the safest way to cross them is as important as learning to abseil. Like the latter it is not intended that the leader should pass on this skill to his own charges, but rather that, fully aware of the dangers, he can make a valid decision to cross or not and that if he decides to cross then the crossing is made safely.

It is perfectly possible to select a safe and suitable section of the river at any time according to its condition. For training purposes several alternative sites should be chosen each with its own indicator to show when the water has reached its optimum height. If the river is too high at one crossing point perhaps a locality

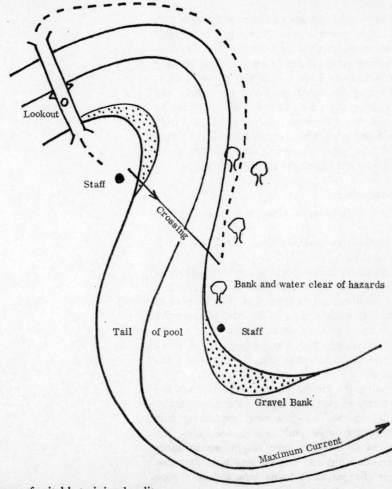

Fig. 3: Diagram of suitable training locality

on a tributary would offer better conditions. Normally, difficulty is experienced in finding water of sufficient depth and pace. In this case the session should be postponed until conditions improve, since much of the point of the exercise will be lost if the crossing is too easy. Where possible the crossing should be made from shallow to deep and from slack to fast moving water with an easy avenue of return either across a bridge or by wide easy shallows. These conditions are commonly found at bends in the river where the form of the river carries the main current to the outside of the bend. The stretch chosen must be free of hazards such as submerged trees, dangerous undertows, high difficult banks and so on and the outflow should be into a quiet pool with a gravelly, shallow tail.

A member of staff should be stationed at this point in case a fielding operation should be necessary. A look-out should also be posted upstream of the crossing to give warning of the approach of any heavy floating debris. Life jackets should be worn by all those actually engaged in crossing the river whenever the rope is not in use.

Training

In mountain areas where there is quick run off of surface rain water into the burns even the smallest streams can become raging torrents in a matter of moments. In this condition they are potentially very dangerous and if there is any doubt at all about whether or not they can be crossed then either make a detour or stay put until the floods subside. This decision is the key to the whole problem. It can only be taken by the party leader on the spot, bearing in mind all the factors relevant to the safety of those in his charge.

If it is considered that the river is fordable, then certain fundamental rules must be observed:

■ Inspect as much of the river as possible before selecting the best crossing point. It is often quite easy to ford a river near its mouth. Mountain burns running into lakes normally flatten out and consequently slow down in the last half mile or so. Generally, the water is quite deep but slow-flowing. Again, however, great care must be taken in crossing, particularly with the non-swimmer.

■ Small and/or light people will be swept off their feet at shallower depths. Make allowances for this when selecting the best crossing point.

■ Packs should be carried high on the back, making sure that any waist belt or head strap is undone for quick release if this should prove necessary. In really fast water, stones or other ballast can be added to the sack to increase stability.

■ Never remove boots even when fording a small burn. For comfort, stockings may be taken off and boots worn on bare feet. Trousers too may be removed to reduce friction.

■ Do not test the force of the water without being secured from the bank.

■ Do not attempt to cross by jumping from boulder to boulder where one slip, so easily done, could result in serious injury.

■ If fording a river which is not in heavy flood it is useful to use a stout stick as a third leg. It must be inserted on the upstream side and can be used as a probe for depth.

■ Never face downstream where the force of the water acting on the back of the legs can cause the knees to give way. Make sure that one foot is firmly placed before moving the other. Do not cross your legs.

■ It can be a great help to angle the hips in such a way that the current exerts a force in the direction of crossing. Adopt a 'ferry-glide' position with the leading hip (i.e. the one nearest the bank you are heading for) advanced to make an angle of up to 45° with the current.

Method using a rope
(*See illustrations overleaf*)

Fig. 4. (i) The leader 'B' ties on to a loop in the rope (figure of eight knot) and sets off across and slightly downstream supporting himself on the rope held by 'A'. He should face upstream at all times. 'A' and 'C' should not be belayed and simply pass the rope through their hands. In the event of 'B' slipping in, he is pulled to the shore by 'C' while 'A' lets his rope run.

Never try to pull a man to the bank from upstream of him. He is certain to be dragged under.

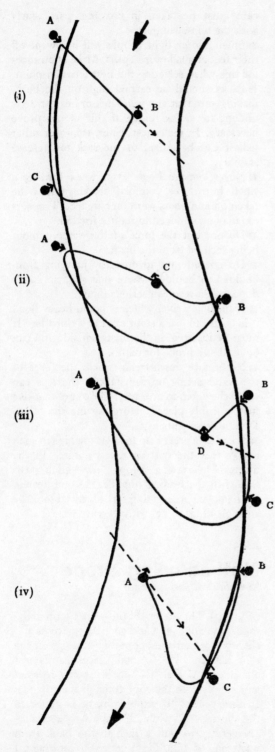

(i)

(ii)

(iii)

(iv)

Fig. 4: Crossing with a rope

(ii) On reaching the far bank 'B' slips off his waist loop but leaves it tied to the rope. 'C' ties on to a second loop and, supported by 'A', who should, if possible, take up a position on a suitable promontory, sets off in the manner described for 'B'. If 'C' should fall in he is pulled to shore by 'B', on the downstream side.

(iii) Once two men are established on the far bank the method can be varied slightly to assist those who come after. 'B' can now take up a position upstream of 'D', crossing, and offer him considerably more support with the rope. Should 'D' fall in he can still be fielded by 'C' on the downstream side.

(iv) The last man crosses in a similar manner to the first, supported by 'B' and pulled in by 'C' if he falls in.

Fig. 5. If two ropes are available the leader and second man may cross as in (i) and (ii) above. The third ('D') and subsequent members of the party tie on to the middle of one rope and the end of the other as shown: Fig. 5. 'D' is supported by both 'A' and 'B' as he crosses diagonally downstream. In the event of a mishap he can be fielded by 'C'. On reaching the far bank he unties and secures the rope from 'B' and 'C' to the 'tail' held by 'A'. 'A' then pulls all the ropes across for the next man.

Fig. 6. Alternative method of getting main body across when high banks or trees permit a single rope to be stretched taut across the river.

The leader 'B' crosses in the manner previously described, tying on to two ropes instead of one.

On reaching the far bank he unties and one of the ropes is stretched taut across the river diagonally downstream as shown and some 10 ft. to 12 ft. above the surface. Any solid anchor can be used, such as a tree or rock, provided it gives sufficient clearance. The rope can be tensioned by 'A' and the remainder of the group using a simple pulley system.

It is important that it should be tight enough not to sag into the water when holding the weight of a man at its mid point.

'C' then ties on to the middle of the second rope held by 'A' and 'B' on opposite banks. He attaches himself to the taut rope by means of a sling (or loop in his safety rope) and karabiner. For stability, he can hold on to the fixed rope and assisted by 'B' makes his way diagonally downstream to join him. The remainder of the party cross in the same way with the exception of the last man who crosses in a similar manner to the first.

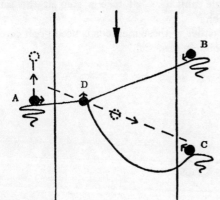

Fig. 5.

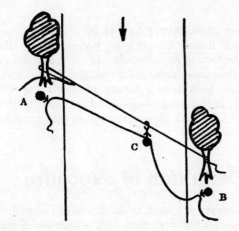

Fig. 6

The method is effective and safe if properly rigged, but is dependent on finding suitable anchors in the right position and high enough above the river. The party must also be carrying two ropes, karabiners and slings.

Method Without a Rope

Only in circumstances of the most dire necessity should any attempt be made to cross a river without a link to the bank. In such circumstances the following methods have proved to be the most successful:

■ Cross in groups of three with arms firmly linked, heads close together and feet apart. The lower man must face upstream and only one must move at a time. In this way the two stationary men can support the moving man.

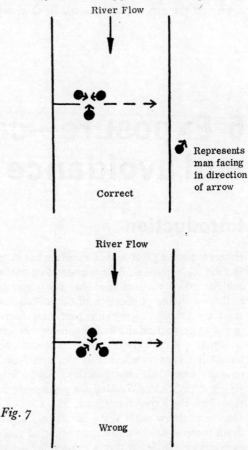

Represents man facing in direction of arrow

Fig. 7

■ A satisfactory alternative method is for three or more to cross in a line downstream thus:

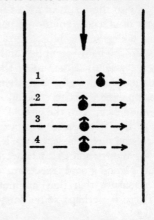

Fig. 8

The first man takes a small step sideways, supported by No. 2 who should be the heaviest in the party. No. 2 steps into line behind him, supported by No. 3 and so on until all the party are in a single line downstream. No. 1 moves again and the process is repeated. In this way the line moves slowly across the stream. In heavy water it is better if the group moves as a single unit (i.e. all take a step at the same time).

If either of these methods is used great care is absolutely essential.

6 Exposure—causes and avoidance

Introduction

In recent years a great deal of attention has been focused on 'exposure'. An understanding of the subject among mountaineers has been greatly facilitated by the publication of the findings of the Outward Bound working party appointed in 1963 to report on the dangers, detection and treatment of exhaustion and exposure on mountains. I am grateful to them for permission to quote from their report in this Chapter and also to Dr. Gordon Waddell for permission to reproduce the Expedition Chart, Fig. 10.

In the past few years there has been a significant increase in the number of reported cases of exposure. No doubt this is in part due to the increased numbers at risk and to improved knowledge leading to recognition of its symptoms, but it is also the result of a vast increase in the number of officially sponsored parties of young people taking to the hills. All too often these youngsters are badly equipped and led by people who are woefully ignorant of the basic rules of mountain safety and who themselves lack the relevant experience to cope adequately with any emergency. On the whole, young people are particularly sensitive to exposure. Their physical and mental reserves are less than adults and for this reason great care must be taken in the planning and execution of any expedition to ensure that they are not overstretched. There is perhaps some danger that our attention may be diverted from the bread and butter business of prevention by the spectacular recommendations on the treatment of exposure cases. Many long cherished cures have been thrown out the window along with St. Bernard dogs, brandy and hot-water bottles. Think ahead. There is no substitute for careful planning.

Definition of exposure

This is not a strict medical term but in general usage it describes the serious effects which may result from exposure to climatic hazards. It is, in general, limited to the effects of cold environments, phrases frequently used including 'suffering from exposure', 'death by exposure', 'risk of exposure'. The essential feature of conditions described in this way is a reduction in the heat content of the body. This becomes serious when deep body temperature begins to fall. So, a definition of exposure to meet the current use of the term is: Severe chilling of the body surface leading to a progressive fall of body temperature with the risk of death from hypothermia.

The importance of exhaustion in the exposure syndrome cannot be overemphasised. It is this factor which distinguishes exposure in the mountains from other forms, such as that suffered by old people in winter in inadequately heated houses or by immersion in the sea. In these cases the cause is almost entirely confined to the cooling effect of the environment. In the mountains, cold alone rarely kills, but when the energy reserves of the body are so depleted that it can no longer maintain deep body temperature, exposure is the sequel.

It is the combination of exhaustion, cold, anxiety or mental stress which is especially dangerous. The elements in this combination will vary greatly with the individual, as will the individual's susceptibility to some or all of these factors. In considering exposure to cold, it is well to bear in mind what has been written by Mr. D. G. Duff, F.R.C.S., himself a mountaineer and rescuer of long experience. 'It is, I consider, the additional factor of physical exhaustion over and above cold which kills quickly. Death has overtaken whole parties who, thinking they must keep moving at all costs, have "bashed on" instead of resting in some shelter before exhaustion supervened. The essential is always to preserve a sufficient reserve of energy in severe conditions of cold and high wind.'

As a rider it may be added that, as with an injured and immobilised climber in the mountains, it is clear that cold may kill a person who is not, as such, physically exhausted. In this condition, however, the climber would certainly be suffering from shock and would therefore be much more susceptible to the effects of cold. Everything should be done to minimise shock and to allay his fears. It is emphasised that the risk of death from exposure is a real, and often unrecognised danger among those, particularly the young, undertaking mountain expeditions in bad weather conditions.

Causes of exposure

The causes of exposure may be divided into two categories: those factors which relate to the *individual* and those which relate to the *environment*.

Environmental Factors

■ In the dry cold environment the factors to be considered are air temperature and wind speed, the combined cooling effect of which is known as wind chill. In Fig. 9, loss of body heat in a normally clothed, stationary person has been plotted for various combinations of air temperature and wind speed. Each of the three lines shown represents a constant level of heat loss. To put it another way, an identical cooling effect can be achieved by different combinations of wind and temperature.

It can be seen that the body loses the same amount of heat when exposed to still air at 32°F (freezing) as it does when exposed to air at 65°F in a 10 m.p.h. wind. The significance of even a small increase in wind speed is clearly seen, particularly in the range 0 – 15 m.p.h. Above this, increases appear to have relatively little effect on cooling. This does not imply that high winds can be discounted in other respects. A great deal of extra energy is obviously required to battle against a 60 m.p.h. wind than a 20 m.p.h. one. In the matter of prevention then, protection of the *whole* body from the wind is important.

■ Most cases of exposure in the mountains of the United Kingdom occur in wet cold conditions and it is astonishing that in a country with such a high annual rainfall more attention has not been directed towards remaining dry. Even the best clothing suffers an enormous loss of its insulating efficiency when it becomes saturated and in a wind, heat loss is further accelerated by convection and evaporation. Complete waterproofing brings its problems, but these can, at least in part, be overcome by good design.

Individual Factors

INSUFFICIENT OR INADEQUATE CLOTHING
It follows from the above that clothing should offer a reasonable degree of independence from the environment. A *waterproof* anorak (and therefore also windproof) is a 'must' and there are many reasonable, cheap, lightweight 'cagoules' on the market. Beware of garments that 'breathe' – few of them stand up to practical testing and in really wet conditions they leak at the seams and under the rucksack straps. If an anorak of this type is worn then a waterproof over-anorak must be carried in the pack. Sweating can be a problem, but the design should allow for a considerable degree of ventilation and this keeps condensation to a minimum. Careful regulation of pace uphill and of the amount of clothing worn helps to avoid discomfort.

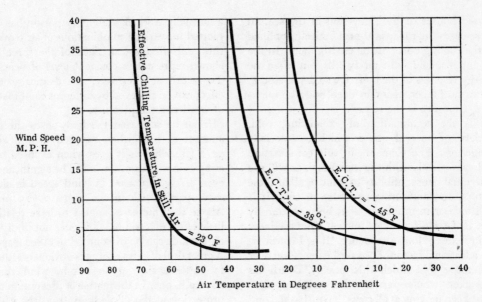

Fig. 9: Wind chill chart

A comprehensive list of clothing and equipment for different expeditions in summer or winter is listed in appendix 'E'. It is however worth drawing attention to the fact that an enormous amount of heat can be lost from the thighs and also from the head, both parts of the body that are all too commonly ignored as far as adequate cover is concerned. Jeans are quite unsuitable for outdoor work and give absolutely no protection in bad weather. The range and design of protective clothing nowadays is such that it is inexcusable for groups to set out inadequately clad. It is the instructor's or leader's responsibility to see that each person in his charge is wearing or carrying sufficient to afford adequate protection in the event of bad weather.

LOWERED RESERVES OF ENERGY
leading to exhaustion. This may be caused either by attempting too much or by not replacing used energy by eating sufficient food. Exhaustion in itself is a dangerous condition since it implies that the body is quite unable to mobilise any further reserves of energy either to do physical work, in other words to carry on, or even to maintain normal body temperature against the sapping of the environment. A man engaged in heavy manual work expends something between 4000 and 4500 Calories per day. The mountain equivalent of this is a 12-mile walk involving 2500 ft. of climbing. In fact a fairly normal sort of mountain day. The calculation is based on a simple formula. (G. Waddell 1965):

$$E = 100 (10 + R + 2C + 4H)$$

where E is the energy expenditure in Kilocalories per 24-hour period; R is the distance travelled on roads in miles per day; C is the distance travelled across country in miles per day; and H is the total height climbed in thousands of feet per day.

Quite clearly, an expenditure of the order of 4400 Calories of energy per day is going to require good training and an adequate food intake especially if this level of output is to be maintained for any length of time, as on an expedition for example. The formula, too, does not make allowance for difficult terrain, weather and load carried, all factors which could add substantially to the total energy demands. There are of course energy reserves available in the body but you cannot go on drawing on them indefinitely – sooner or later they have to be topped up by a period of rest and recuperation. A good balanced diet providing about 4000+ Calories per day is essential and this should include a high energy lunch snack to be taken on the hill in addition to the personal emergency ration which of course must be kept in reserve. Over a period of time routes and expeditions should be planned so as to avoid making excessive overall demands, especially on young people. Start in a modest way with expeditions in the 2400 – 2800 Calorie Requirement (CR) range and gradually build up to more ambitious projects. Exhaustion is always a possibility, but it becomes a probability if routes in excess of 4500 CR are tackled without adequate preparation and training. Know the individual capabilities of your party and plan accordingly.

The estimation of time to be allowed is of vital importance both in navigation and in route planning. Naismith's rule has for long been enshrined in mountain lore as the basis for all these calculations – and rightly so since it gives approximately the right answer for an average party on an average day, i.e. 3 m.p.h. plus ½ hour for each 1000 ft. climbed. However, it takes no account of terrain, weather, load carried, fitness, and the effect of fatigue at the end of a long day. In fact for short or long trips it is wildly out. Recent modifications to Naismith's rule have attempted to take account of as many of these variables as possible. The results of this work are tabulated below (Tranter 1965).

The left-hand column represents varying degrees of fitness or condition (with the fittest at the top) as measured by the time taken when fresh to climb 1000 ft. in ½ mile at a 'normal' pace and without rests. Once the individual fitness rating is known or estimated it is possible to read off from the chart the 'corrected' value for any time calculated on the basis of Naismith's rule. Other adjustments are necessary to take account of the remaining variables.

■ Distance on Roads: in calculating time according to Naismith's rule work on the basis of 4 m.p.h.

■ Load Carried: drop one 'fitness' line from the one normally used for each 35 lbs. carried.

■ Terrain: drop one or two 'fitness' lines

Corrections to Naismith's Rule

Individual Fitness in Minutes	*Time taken in hours calculated according to Naismith's rule*															
	2	3	4	5	6	7	8	9	10	12	14	16	18	20	22	24
15	1	1½	2	2¾	3½	4½	5½	6¾	7¾	10	12½	14½	17	19½	22	24
20	1¼	2¼	3¼	4½	5½	6½	7¾	8¾	10	12½	15	17½	20	23		
25	1½	3	4¼	5½	7	8½	10	11½	13¼	15	17½					
30	2	3½	5	6¾	8½	10½	12½	14½								
40	2¾	4¼	5¾	7½	9½	11½										
50	3¼	4¾	6½	8½												

Too much to be attempted

Limit Line

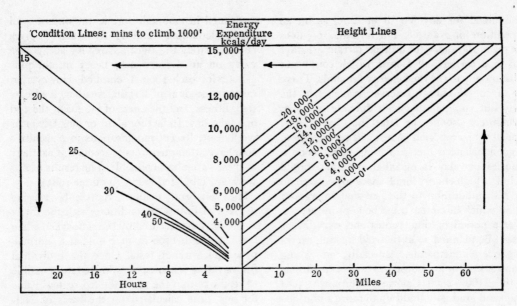

Fig. 10: Expedition time chart

according to the nature of the ground. Under snow the time taken varies enormously, depending on its state at the time. Once this has been established drop 1 – 4 'condition' lines as appropriate.

■ Weather: drop one 'fitness' line at night or in bad visibility or if strong winds are present. If strong head winds are forecast for the return journey drop two 'condition' lines.

This rather involved process of arriving at a fair estimate of the time required for any particular journey has been neatly summarised in the chart – Fig. 10. (Aldridge, Waddell, Tranter.) Start at the bottom right-hand side of the chart with the 'corrected mileage', i.e. the total mileage across country plus three-quarters of the total distance on roads. Follow the arrow vertically until you intersect with the line representing the total height climbed. From this intersection move horizontally towards the centre line and read off the Energy expenditure. Continue leftwards to meet your particular 'Fitness' line; adjusted of course to take account of the factors previously mentioned, i.e. Load, Terrain and Weather. If you run out of 'Fitness' lines it can be assumed that conditions are too severe. If you do not meet your line because it stops short the trip must also be regarded as too

arduous. From this point descend vertically to the base line to read the estimated time in hours.

DEHYDRATION

Perhaps because water is so plentiful in Britain we tend to ignore the fact that it is a vital ingredient of the diet. The normal turnover is about 4 pints per day, but in a hot climate and when engaged in hard physical work it can rise to five times this amount. There is a general reluctance among walkers and climbers to take water on the hill. This seems to be due to vague fears of pollution, stomach cramps and other debilitating effects, most of which are imaginary. Water is required and the more work done, the more water is necessary. Roughly speaking about $\frac{3}{4}$ pint is required for each 1000 kilocalories of energy expended in winter and about double this in summer. The 12-mile mountain walk involving 2500 ft. of ascent previously referred to has a CR value of 4400 and a water requirement in summer of $6\frac{3}{4}$ pints. It is of course possible to go into water debt and replenish stocks at the end of the day, but if the expedition is a long one this could be a dangerous policy. It is better to keep pace with the needs of the body and drink when the opportunity presents itself, 'little and often' being the best maxim to follow. On a long expedition salt lost through sweating should also be replaced to avoid muscle cramp. Serious dehydration leads to a decrease in physical and mental efficiency and lowers resistance to exhaustion.

LACK OF TRAINING AND CONDITIONING

The importance of training and of a gradual build up towards more ambitious expeditions has already been stressed. Overestimation of fitness and underestimation of time are all too common causes of accidents. Where large groups are concerned it is obviously better to arrange people into fitness groups according to their condition times than to cater for all on the basis of the lowest common denominator. The latter policy, apart from being bad for the morale of all concerned, leads to the dangerous situation whereby the weak can be pushed too far and the strong barely kept at 'tick-over'.

In addition to improving the physical performance of individuals, training should be designed to familiarise the group with the range of difficult conditions which may be expected and in this way condition them to a certain extent both mentally and physically against hardship and discomfort. Such conditioning is of proven value in cold climates and there is no doubt that it helps to maintain a high level of morale in our own.

MORALE

This is something of an unknown quantity. Certainly it cannot be measured and yet it is one of the most significant contributory factors to exposure. Apprehension, fear and a spirit of hopelessness can induce a state akin to shock and if not checked can spread through a party like a bush fire. Confident and cheerful leadership should be the keynote with a wary eye and ear for the first sign of depression or panic. This does not mean that in a tricky situation the leader should pretend that everything in the garden is lovely but rather that he should inspire the confidence and the willingness to co-operate among his charges that is necessary for a successful outcome.

INJURY

Shock is present to some degree in every case of injury and it is important to treat the patient for this as well as for his injuries. A person in a state of shock is much less able to combat the effects of cold and maintain his body temperature. He is in fact half way towards exposure already and must be protected from the environment by all means at your disposal.

7 Exposure—recognition and treatment

Symptoms of exposure

It is not always easy to decide early enough that you have a mild case of exposure on your hands. It is very important to do so, since it may be possible to avoid a crisis if at the outset you are aware of the symptoms and can begin to treat them. This makes it incumbent on the leader to know his party sufficiently well to be able to recognise genuinely uncharacteristic behaviour when it arises.

The following are among the symptoms:

■ Unexpected and apparently unreasonable behaviour, often accompanied by complaints of coldness and tiredness.

■ Physical and mental lethargy, including

failure to respond to or to understand questions and directions.

■ Failure of, or abnormality in vision. It should be noted that some failure of vision is a very usual symptom, and when this does occur, the condition should be regarded with extreme seriousness.

■ Some slurring of speech. There is not necessarily early *failure* of speech and victim may speak quite strongly until shortly before collapse.

■ Sudden shivering fits.

■ Violent outbursts of unexpected energy – possible physical resistance to succour – violent language.

■ Falling.

N.B. It should be stressed that not all of these symptoms may be noticed, nor necessarily in this order. Other symptoms which may sometimes be observed are muscle cramp, extreme ashen pallor, light-headedness, occasionally a fainting fit.

Treatment

General

In normal conditions the inner 'core' (trunk and brain) of the body remains constant at 37°C (98·4°F): the temperature of the outer shell consisting of the skin, underlying fat and muscle, and extremities (arms and legs, ears, nose) is always below this.

What is vital is the preservation of the deep core temperature. A shift in this leads directly to *mental deterioration and loss of muscular co-ordination, and eventually to unconsciousness, heart and respiratory failure and death.*

The body itself acts to maintain core circulation and temperature by restricting the flow to the exposed periphery so that core blood is not cooled at the surface.

In any treatment, therefore, the importance must be realised of not increasing peripheral circulation unless there is minimal loss of heat at the skin surface, further heat loss from the core must at all costs be avoided, sudden local surface warming therefore is wrong.

When once the symptoms are clearly established, any further exertion, such as forcing the victim to go on walking, even downhill, must be avoided. The party must stop, and proceed to treatment. *It is impossible to overstress the importance of this.*

Immediate Treatment in the Field

As already indicated, the risk of precipitating a sudden surge of circulation to the surface, such as may be produced by hot water bottles / rubbing / or alcohol intake, should be avoided.

The precipitation of a sudden surge of core blood can be disastrous, as this blood is cooled by going through the cold outer shell, and is then returned to the heart.

The essential and immediate treatment is to prevent further heat loss by insulating the body and to use every means available to make a positive contribution to the heat balance of the victim.

Methods will vary according to conditions and the equipment immediately available. An outline of what should be done, if at all possible is:

■ If plenty of dry insulation is available remove the victim's wet clothes, dry him, and get him into a sleeping bag. If this is impracticable, wrap him in sleeping bags to provide insulation below as well as above his body.

■ Put a fit companion into the sleeping bag alongside him, to give him bodily warmth. This treatment is effective only if there is skin to skin contact and therefore both victim and companion must be stripped.

■ There should be a windproof and waterproof covering (e.g. polythene) around the bag and the victim. The insulation between him and the ground is the most important of all.

■ Try to provide some shelter as windbreak.

■ Meanwhile, get the rest of the party to pitch a tent over the victim to provide fuller shelter. If the tent has a sewn-in groundsheet, carry him inside the tent. Light a stove if carried and get as many people inside as possible, but ensure adequate ventilation.

■ If the victim can still take food, sugar in easily digestible form (e.g. condensed milk) may be given. A warm sweet drink may be prepared later if available.

■ If respiration ceases, perform artificial respiration continuously by mouth to nose / mouth method.

■ Be alert for failure of the heart (no pulse, blue lips, dilated pupils) and commence cardiac massage immediately. If necessary a second person can continue resuscitation at the rate of one inflation after every five compressions.

There will then normally ensue a period perhaps of some hours duration, before the rescue party with stretcher that has been summoned can arrive. Even if, during this period, the patient apparently recovers, and even if he insists that he is quite fit, he must still be treated as a stretcher-case, however unwilling or ashamed he may be, and the full normal rescue drill must be enforced. During this waiting period, once the patient has been insulated, a brew-up should be started, and hot beverages and food should be given to him, according to what he can take. Food and hot drinks should also be taken by those members of the party who have remained with him, and whom it is safer to regard as themselves suffering in some degree from shock and exhaustion.

The stretcher party, when it arrives, should of course preserve all the insulation around the patient, during the carry, with which he has been protected during the waiting period. It is important that his face and mouth should be protected, to minimise heat-loss, without interfering with ventilation and ease of breathing. It is imperative that in descent the patient should be evacuated in the head down position and that someone (not a stretcher bearer) is detailed to keep an eye on him in case of vomiting, respiratory or cardiac failure.

If a case of exposure occurs in a very distant and isolated spot, and the delay before the arrival of the rescue party is likely to be inordinately long, the instructor or leader may face the very difficult decision as to whether to start removing the casualty towards the rescuers and safety. But before any such attempt is made, all the measures of immediate treatment in the field, as outlined above, should be taken first. And only if considerations of time, distance, and bad weather then clearly make it less of a risk to carry the patient towards safety, than to keep him, insulated and cared for, where he is, should the risk of carrying him be accepted.

This emphasises the real need for all instructors and leaders in charge of a party to be trained not only in up-to-date First Aid methods, including mouth to nose resuscitation, but also to be expert in the safest carrying techniques that may be attempted without a proper stretcher.

Recommended Treatment at Base

If it can be done, rapid rewarming by total immersion in a hot bath between 113°F and 117°F or 45°C and 47°C is a proved lifesaver. A bath thermometer is a useful thing to have available, otherwise judge the safe heat as being the hottest temperature in which you can keep an elbow in the water. A bed and room should be warmed while the bath is being prepared. Strip the patient, at least of wet outer garments, and immerse in the bath taking care to exclude any frostbitten part. This should be dealt with separately (see Chapter 15). The legs too may be left out (Gramminger) since a suffusion of blood in that direction may dangerously reduce the blood volume. The bath temperature will drop immediately and therefore it must be topped up with hot water at regular intervals. After 20 minutes, or when the patient begins to sweat, remove him in the prone position (do not sit him up) and transfer to the previously warmed bed. Recovery is often spectacularly misleading. Insist on complete rest and examination by a doctor as a matter of urgency.

Such sophisticated facilities will not be available in a base camp. However, much the same effect can be achieved in a superheated tent (ensure adequate ventilation) and by immersing both hands in a billy of water brought to the same temperature (113°F – 117°F).

There is no doubt that rapid rewarming, effective though it has proved, involves a certain degree of risk, especially for the unconscious, the very old and the very young and in others who for one reason or another are frail or unwell. It is suggested that in such cases spontaneous rewarming in a warm room and bed (no pillow) should be the treatment of choice.

Conclusion

It is said that an Eskimo, immersed in cold Arctic water, will die from hypothermia (cooling) just as quickly as the rest of us. His ability, not only to survive, but to live comfortably in a hostile environment is almost entirely due to the fact that he keeps fit, dresses well and is highly experienced in avoidance. This, perhaps slightly unfair comparison, sums up all that is necessary to know as regards prevention. Better by far that you should know how to avoid getting a case of exposure than to cure one. Therefore:

■ See to it that the equipment and clothing worn by the party is sufficient for the route chosen and takes cognisance of sudden and unexpected changes in conditions. Water-proofing is a must whether it be worn or carried in the pack.

■ A minimum of emergency food and equipment must be carried by the party. A suggested list may be found in Appendix E.

■ Adequate food and water should be taken before and during any mountain journey.

■ Progressive training is important as is the careful regulation of pace throughout the day. Arrange large groups according to their fitness and capabilities.

■ Loads in excess of 40 lbs. are unnecessary, as well as being heavy. As a rough guide on a camping expedition loads should never exceed one-third of the body weight of the individual.

■ Good morale means increased safety.

■ Safety first – seek shelter or turn back in good time.

■ Good leadership is good planning.

Finally it must be said that good leadership is also an awareness on the part of the leader of each member of his party as an individual; an awareness amounting almost to a premonition of possible hazards and dangers that may arise and above all the ability to take avoiding action before circumstances dictate their own terms.

8 Weather

The British Isles, unlike many other parts of the world, are so notorious for the inconsistency of their weather, that it is essential to accept the fact that regardless of season, anything might happen. 'Summer' days, with cold northerly blasts and flurries of snow in the hills or glorious days in mid-winter, when the unwary are tempted to dress lightly and are ill-prepared for a sudden change, are commonplace.

The constant interchange of Tropical and Polar air masses is the cause of the sometimes dramatic weather changes over these islands but it is the birth of fronts and depressions, where these air masses meet, that leads to the rapid succession of daily changes.

In this kind of situation, it is no easy task for the amateur forecaster to give reliable predictions; nor is it even possible for the professional, with all aids at his disposal, to be consistently accurate, particularly as the 'regions' of his forecasts sometimes cover wide geographical areas. On the other hand, accuracy is possible for the amateur on the spot, who can recognise and apply to the wider situation, signs of changing weather.

The subject of 'Weather' cannot be adequately treated in one brief chapter nor even in one book can the treatment be comprehensive. It is a vast study and forecasting requires years of theoretical and practical work but, for Certificate purposes, it is of vital importance that mountain leaders are, if no more, at least aware of weather terms and their implications and that they give due recognition to these in their plans.

Fairly up-to-date weather maps showing

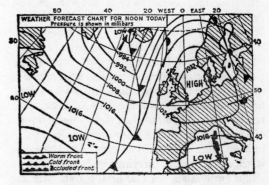

Fig. 11: Anticyclone

pressure distribution are screened daily by the British Broadcasting Corporation Television Service and others, although a bit outdated, are printed in some national newspapers.

Figure 11 shows an anti-cyclone or a large area of High Pressure, centred slightly to the east of the British Isles. This type of pressure distribution, shown by isobars or lines joining up places with the same air pressure, brings fairly static weather conditions. Light winds blowing in a clockwise direction and even dead calms are characteristic and changes, when they occur, do so slowly and usually over a period of days. Cloudless skies are often associated with anti-cyclones but overcast conditions are not infrequent. In both summer and winter, over-night temperature inversions are fairly common and particularly in sheltered inland valleys there are often frosts and fog.

Conditions in a Ridge of High Pressure (Fig. 12) are not unlike those in an anti-cyclone but they are normally of shorter duration. Particularly in a fast moving ridge it is possible to locate one's approximate position by reference to the wind direction and by this means crude estimations of further changes can be made.

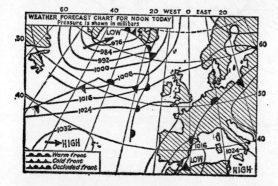

Fig. 12: Ridge of high pressure

Air that remains in contact with the earth's surface gradually acquires properties, notably temperature and humidity, of the underlying surface. The regions where these air masses are found are called air mass sources. As in anti-cyclones air flows out gently in a clockwise direction and this forms the airstreams which together account for a large part of British weather.

The four major sources and the characteristics of the airstreams are:

■ *Maritime Tropical* S.W. winds fairly steady. Warm and moist, even in winter. Stratus cloud forms on the West side of mountains often with rain or drizzle but generally the weather is clear and dry on the lee side.

■ *Continental Tropical* Winds S. or S.S.E. Hot and dry. Very poor visibility in summer. Clear skies but hazy. This airstream is not common but it can bring very high winter temperatures.

■ *Maritime Polar* N.W. winds. Cold in winter and cool in summer. It is an unstable airstream with showers developing frequently particularly to windward of mountain ranges. Cumulus and cumulo-nimbus cloud form is typical. Except in showers there is very good visibility.

■ *Continental Polar* North and north-east winds. The weather is cold and dry. Conditions are unstable and therefore showery with cumulus clouds but the air lacks moisture and in winter the phenomenon of ablation is common (i.e. snow falling but apparently disappearing as it reaches the ground).

The depression is an area of low pressure relative to the surrounding air. It is difficult to catalogue the associated weather as this varies particularly with the size. There are, for example, on the one hand, many large slow moving depressions which linger long enough to establish airstreams on their margins.

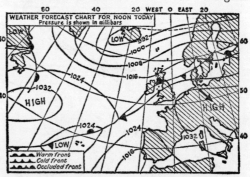

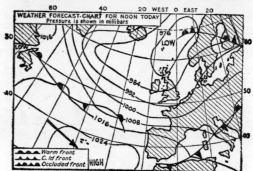

Figs. 13 and 14: Maritime airstream

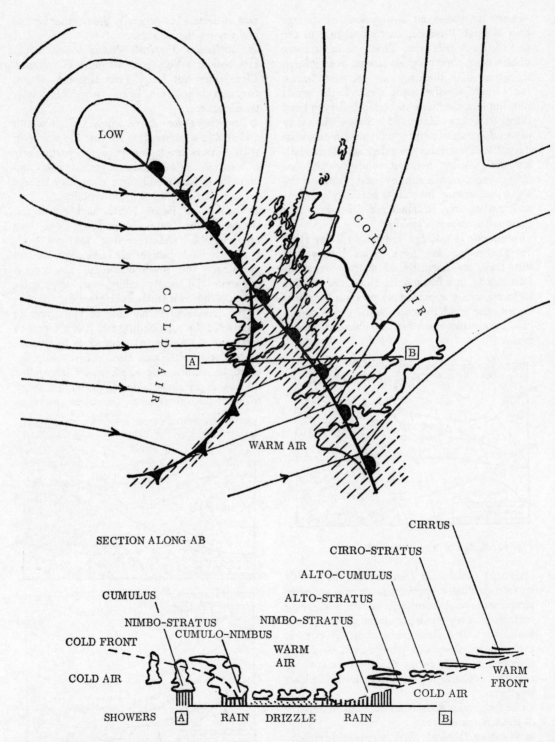

Fig. 15: Depression with fronts

On the other hand, some of the smaller depressions or lows, usually with associated fronts, move quickly and they generally exhibit certain features of cloud, wind, temperature and humidity which are easily recognisable.

The winds in all depressions in the northern hemisphere blow anti-clockwise and slightly inwards across the isobars. From the diagram shown above it can be seen that if an observer stands back to the wind, low pressure is on the left. This is always true and is an aid to determining the observer's position in relation to pressure distribution.

By observing wind direction, it is possible to recognise various stages in the passage of fronts and of the depression. If, for example, a depression moving from west to east passes over an observer the sequence of wind change would show a veering to the west as the warm front passed and to the north west with the passage of the cold front. If, on the other hand, the track of the low was from S.W. to N.E. then the initial wind would be south east followed by light winds and then a sudden veer to the N.W.

The passage of fronts is heralded by cloud change. Well ahead of a warm front, small wisps of cirrus increase in amount, developing into a veil of cirrostratus. With this type of cloud the phenomenon of a halo round the sun or moon is not uncommon. Closer to the front, the medium height cloud thickens and falls to a lower altitude. This altostratus cloud continues to thicken and eventually, as rain begins to fall, it becomes nimbostratus (rainstratus). As the warm front passes, the surface wind veers and frequently stops or gives place to a drizzle. At this stage it is not unusual for the stratus cloud to break up and expose clear sky although low stratus cloud with continuous light drizzle is equally possible. The passage of the cold front is marked by a fall in temperature. The wind backs to north-west and simultaneously cloud cover breaks to expose blue sky. The cloud form is cumulus and alto cumulus and precipitation is in the form of showers.

The passage of a cold front alone or of a warm front is equally possible but over Britain much of the rain which falls does so in association with an occluded front, i.e. the final stage in the evolution of fronts where a cold front advancing on a warm front lifts up the warm air mass above ground level (Figures 16, 17). An occlusion frequently shows increasing cloud cover similar to the approach of a warm front but rainfall is generally less with lighter winds. The belt of rain associated with a cold occlusion is usually narrower than with the warm type.

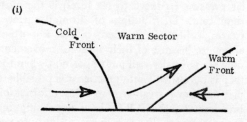

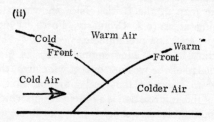

Fig. 16

In Figure 16 the air in advance of the warm front is colder than the air in the rear of the cold front and a warm occlusion results.

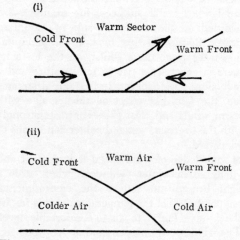

Fig. 17

In Figure 17, with the colder air to the rear of the cold front, the occlusion is said to be a cold occlusion. In this case, which is the more common, the temperature falls as the occlusion passes.

■ There are internationally recognised symbols for use on official weather maps although the simpler versions used in newspapers and on television use very few of these. The isobar, or the line on the map connecting places with equal air pressure (reduced to sea level) is the most significant. Distribution of frontal surfaces (warm, cold and occluded) is also important although, because of their speed of movement, they are normally well out of position when the map is published. With practice it is possible to plot one's own weather map using information broadcast on the B.B.C. long wave shipping forecast service. For this purpose ability to use International Symbols on a pre-constructed outline map of the British Isles showing the shipping areas (e.g. Cromarty, Forth, Tyne, Dogger, etc.) is a prerequisite.

■ Although maps and regional forecasts give knowledge of the weather over a wide area, the ability to interpret the local situation in the light of this information is a practical skill which all mountain leaders should cultivate. Recognition of various cloud forms and appreciation of the significance of wind and even temperature changes all contribute to a better understanding.

■ It is also, of course, essential to interpret the weather situation and the immediate developments in relation to the altitude and the form of the land. Frontal surfaces, for example, are retarded on the windward side of mountain ranges. Because of this, most of the precipitation takes place there whilst, on the lee side, there is generally a rise in temperature and a reduction in windspeeds. In unstable airstreams too, the föhn-like effect on the lee side with warm winds and clear skies contrasts strongly with the overcast, wet and colder conditions to windward.

■ Knowledge of wind speed is important and vitally so in winter conditions where even a light breeze can reduce the environmental temperature (i.e. the temperature as it is felt by the human body) to an uncomfortable level. The wind speed on open land above 3,000 feet is about two to two-and-a-half times stronger than on more sheltered low lying land and, for example, a strong breeze of 23 to 27 miles per hour, at the higher open altitude would become a gale or storm of 50 to 60 miles per hour.

■ Environmental temperature is also affected by humidity. The 'raw' conditions of winter and the 'mugginess' or 'oppression' of a sultry summer's day are all too common. At the other end of the scale, the dessicating effect of a south easterly airflow on both individuals and the land should not be ignored.

■ It is generally known that temperature decrease is from 3°F to 5°F per 1000 feet of ascent dependent on the humidity of the air but it is often forgotten that in anti-cyclones and in stable air streams, temperature inversions and sometimes fog can create very unpleasant camping conditions. In locating an overnight camp it is also worth bearing in mind that east facing slopes in deep north-south valleys catch no early morning sun.

■ Although thunderstorms are not common in the Scottish hills, the mountain leader should be able to recognise a developing thunderstorm. The growth of a dark cumulus congested cloud is generally the first warning. The wind then freshens during its approach, blowing at first towards the oncoming storm. As the thundercloud arrives overhead, the wind begins to blow out from the cloud in a forward direction but before this stage parties should have retreated from the mountain tops. (See Chapter 9.)

9 Lightning

Lightning can hardly be regarded as a major mountain hazard yet every year it claims the lives of two or three mountaineers. Like the winter avalanche it is commonly regarded as an Act of God and the very impartiality by which it chooses its victims encourages a fatalistic outlook among climbers and walkers. The actual physical process is now fairly well understood and this emphasises that there are certain simple precautions which can be taken to avoid a strike.

The first thing to realise is that to be 'struck' by lightning is by no means always fatal. True, a direct hit is likely to be so, but more often than not the victim receives only a part of the stroke, either by induction because he happens to be standing near, or through the ground in the form of earth currents which dissipate like the roots of a tree, from the source. Such partial shocks need not be fatal though they could, of course, cause death indirectly if the climber should fall off or be rendered incapable of fending for himself. The stroke itself is a variable quantity, being a product of a very large current (thousands of amps) and a very short time (thousandths of a second). In many cases a much smaller current in contact for a few seconds could cause considerably more damage.

Fortunately there is usually some advance warning of the approach of an electrical storm and avoiding action can be taken, but once in the firing line decisions tend to be taken out of your hands. Anyone who has experienced the literally hair-raising preliminaries will vouch for this. Ice axes hum and spark, the skin tingles and local projections glow with a bluish light.

During a storm strikes tend to be concentrated on mountain tops or other natural projections from the general surroundings. At the same time, since such points 'service' a fairly wide area, there tends to be a shaded or relatively safe zone associated with them. The peak must be at least 20 ft. high and the relatively safe zone is of the same order horizontally (Fig. 19). Note that it affords no protection to be tucked in against the cliff or peak itself since in this position you are likely to receive earth currents shed from the peak.

Frequency of Strokes:

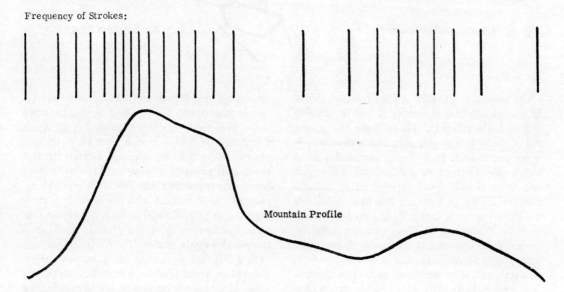

Mountain Profile

Fig. 18: Frequency of 'strokes' in mountain area

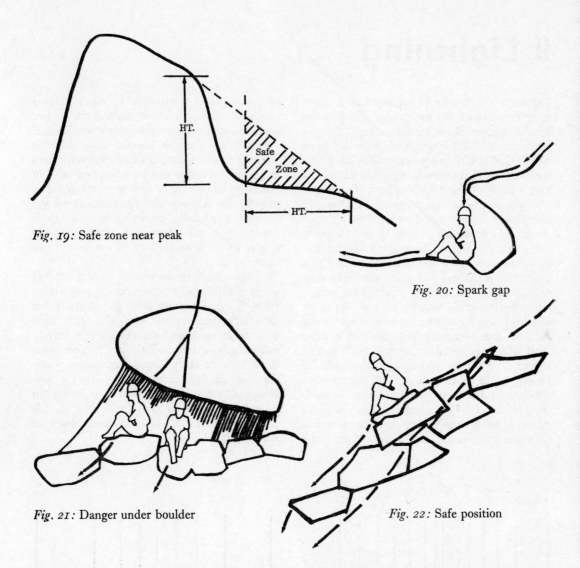

Fig. 19: Safe zone near peak

Fig. 20: Spark gap

Fig. 21: Danger under boulder

Fig. 22: Safe position

The natural inclination in a really heavy storm is to seek shelter, especially if rain is driving down. Unfortunately, this is quite the wrong thing to do unless you can find a cave which gives you at least 10 ft. head room and 4 ft. to either side. Such caves and hollows in the rock are often simply local expansions of natural fissures. These in turn are the likely conduits for earth currents, especially if they hold water and by sheltering in them you are offering yourself as a convenient alternative to the spark gap. (Figs. 20 and 21).

Exactly the same argument applies to sheltering under large boulders. With reasonable waterproof equipment remaining dry should not be a major problem and it is much safer to sit it out in the open. Try to find a broken scree slope, preferably in a safe zone and sit on top of a *dry* rope or rucksack with your knees up and your hands in your lap (Fig. 22). Do not attempt to support yourself on your hands or by leaning back. The object of these precautions is to keep your points of contact with the ground as close together as possible and in such a position that a current flowing along the ground would tend to pass through a non-vital part of the body.

On a cliff face sit out the storm on the nearest ledge, but avoid chimneys and fissures of any kind. If a belay is necessary, try to avoid using the wet rope as a natural lead from a vertical crack to your body. On an exposed peak or ridge your position is much more serious and it is normally advisable to make some attempt to get at least part way down even at the height of the storm. Abseiling in an electrical storm is a risky manoeuvre, but it is normally preferable to a position on the lightning highway of an exposed ridge. In any event, one or two rope lengths may well take you to a position of relative safety. If you do abseil, use a dry rope if you have the choice and use a safety rope. Fatal accidents have often resulted from a non-fatal strike which in the first instance has merely stunned the victim.

It is fashionable, too, to discard pieces of extraneous equipment; cameras, rucksacks, crampons and even ice axes, under the mistaken impression that they 'attract' lightning. They don't, any more than you do yourself. The electrical resistance of the average wooden shafted axe between head and spike is almost five times that of the human body. If it is humming and sparking it may be prudent to lay it down carefully beside you, but no more. The axe is much too valuable a tool to be tossed away in a storm. It may well be needed to deal with icy rocks on the retreat.

10 Mountain rescue

If you are the leader of a party involved in an accident

■ *Don't rush.* See to it that no immediate danger threatens the victim or the rest of the party.
■ *Render immediate first aid* and reassure the victim and the remainder of the party.
■ *Make the victim as comfortable as possible* and provide warmth and shelter as far as circumstances and equipment allow. Be particularly careful to provide adequate insulation from the ground. Provided the victim is not suffering from a spinal injury it may be advantageous to move him to a more sheltered site. If this is not possible then build shelter round him.
■ *Decide on your course of action.* In making your decision weigh carefully the following factors:
The nature of the victim's injuries / The state of the remainder of the party / The time available / The weather situation / The availability of assistance / The evacuation route.
■ *Attempt to attract local assistance using recognised distress signals:*
Red flares (miniflare etc.).

S.O.S. – 3 short, 3 long, 3 short flashes of torch or whistle blasts.
Distress signal – 6 long flashes or blasts in quick succession – repeat after 1 minute.
■ *Send a messenger for help or, if a party of two, go yourself.*
The messenger should carry a written note giving: precise location of the accident – six-figure map reference and compass bearings from known landmarks (if on a climb, the name of the climb and whether near the top or bottom); time of accident; number involved; injuries sustained.
If the victim is to be left on his own he must be told to 'stay put' at all costs. He should be given all the spare food and clothing and provided with a whistle and torch if these are not required by the messenger. Mark the spot clearly with a flag – a brightly coloured garment held on top of a cairn of stones. The climbing or safety rope, if not otherwise required, may be extended out from the victim to act as a marker guide. Remember that the rescue party may have to find the exact spot in the mist or in the dark and in winter the victim may well be covered with drifting snow. An unconscious patient must never be left alone. If a party of two, it is safer for the uninjured person to stay

with the victim to render help when necessary and to attempt to attract the attention of other climbers and walkers. Only as an absolute last resort should the victim be left and in that event he should be tied securely to the rock if in an exposed situation and a note left explaining what action has been taken.

Or

■ *Arrange to evacuate patient(s) yourself, improvising equipment as necessary.*

At the outset it should be remembered that improvised 'carrys' and 'stretchers' are of short range value. It would be exhausting and possibly dangerous to attempt a long evacuation by such methods. Their main use is in moving an injured person to a more sheltered situation or in evacuating someone with relatively minor injuries or, of course, when evacuation by any method is preferable to leaving the victim where he is.

Organisation of search

It is not expected that candidates for the Certificate will be concerned with the organisation of a major search and rescue operation. This is the responsibility of the local team leader in co-operation with the police. Nevertheless it is important that they should have a clear understanding of the system so that they can offer competent assistance in an emergency, perhaps as the leader of a smaller search unit.

Big searches are costly affairs, in terms of man hours as well as in hard cash. An efficient organisation makes the best use of all available resources, minimises delays and frustrations and greatly increases the chances of a successful outcome. Just as it is vital that each small group should have its appointed leader so it is vital that an experienced mountaineer should take overall responsibility for the control and conduct of the search. In a large scale operation this can only be successfully done from a fixed base in contact with all aspects of the search, both in the field and behind the lines.

1 Interview the person bringing the news of the accident. This is best done away from the crowd which invariably gathers at the mention of the word accident. On no account rely on second-hand information. This may be coloured and omit some vital piece of information concerning the circumstances.

2 Establish precise details of the accident, including location, time, number involved and the nature of the injuries.

3 Once this information has been given act *Speedily – Not Hastily. Inform the Local Police and Doctor.* He will make arrangements for an ambulance, but will require an indication of the expected time of arrival back at the roadhead.

4 Each area has devised its own call out system, but it is worth remembering that it is better to have a team on 'stand by' if there is any likelihood of their being required, than to call them out at the very last moment without warning.

5 No two search and rescue operations are ever the same and therefore the *plan* must be adapted to the circumstances. It should be drawn up immediately, again in consultation with the team leaders and the police. Contact the Meteorological Office for an up-to-date weather forecast and inform team leaders.

It is important that:

■ Team leaders are fully briefed on the circumstances of the accident and the responsibilities of their groups. Check on the experience and personal equipment of their members. Radio call signs and an agreed communications system should be established.

■ A record is kept, giving the names of the members of each party and their leader, the route to be followed, special equipment carried, radio call sign, time out, and expected time of return. This information could be of vital importance if a claim on insurance is to be made.

■ Each party should carry sufficient equipment to render positive assistance to any casualties, i.e. (i) first aid kit (ii) spare clothing (iii) food and drink (iv) the means to provide adequate shelter. Other equipment carried will obviously depend on the circumstances known about the accident.

■ *Night Search.* It is hazardous and a waste of man power to send all parties out on a general search at night unless fairly precise information is available. However, some immediate effort must be made and this should take the form of checking mountain huts and other known refuge points.

6 The Search

If the locality is known:

■ Send a small party ahead with an emergency first aid pack. Check that the morphia is in it, and that flares or radio sets are carried. This small first aid pack should contain sufficient materials to deal with most injuries. There is also tremendous psychological value in having help arrive as quickly as possible. If the stretcher party is inexperienced, as is probable, it is better to have the patients tidied up before the party arrives.

■ Organise a stretcher party to follow up the advance party. This should be at least twelve but preferably eighteen persons. Ensure that all members are properly clad and equipped. If there is any doubt, they should not be allowed to proceed.

If the locality is unknown, but the general area fairly well defined:

The stretcher(s) and other heavy gear should be left at some convenient advanced base where it is reasonably accessible to the various units. This base may be moved as the search progresses. Some teams, of course, will be carrying lightweight stretchers.

Three main methods of search are recognised and their use obviously depends on the number of searchers available, their experience, the nature of the ground and information available to the controller.

RECONNAISSANCE SEARCH

Small fast units consisting of three or four experienced men are sent out with the minimum of gear, with the object of locating the casualty as quickly as possible. Helicopters and dogs are tremendously useful in this sort of preliminary scouting operation and may save endless work later.

BLOCK SEARCH

This is the normal method of covering a fairly large area. Each team is allotted a piece of ground bounded if possible by natural features such as streams or ridges. It is then up to the team leader to choose the detailed method of search best suited to the terrain in his area. In most cases this will involve some sort of sweep in line across the area.

CONTACT SEARCH

This method, as the name implies, is designed to concentrate the search over a relatively small area, perhaps at the foot of a cliff or in an area where there is good reason to believe that the missing person may be found. The spacing between searchers is dictated by the ground and may vary from 50 yards in open country to one yard in thick bush. The important point to bear in mind is that this type of search should be conclusive. An area searched in this way must be clearly marked.

HELICOPTERS

These can be of immense value but their use is dependent on reasonable overhead conditions. When lives are at stake, sympathetic consideration is always given by the Service authorities to a request for a helicopter. Any such request should be made through the Police who will contact the Rescue Co-ordination Centre.

Here are some ways in which a ground party can assist the pilot:

■ Clear a level landing zone (LZ) approximately 20 yds. × 20 yds. of all loose material, sticks, etc.

■ Normally the clothing of the ground party should be sufficient to attract the attention of the pilot. If a marker of any kind is used it should be pegged down firmly in the centre of the LZ.

■ Indicate wind direction by releasing a smoke cartridge in such a position that it is on the

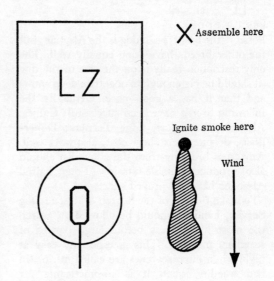

Fig. 23: Helicopter landing zone

pilot's right hand side as he approaches the LZ upwind. Ensure that the smoke will not obscure the LZ. If smoke is not available, then: stand with back to wind and arms outstretched facing the approach path, and shine a torch or headlamp into the wind, i.e. away from the approaching helicopter.

■ The ground party must assemble on the right hand side of the approach path and well clear of the LZ.

■ Approach the helicopter at 45° from in front and on the pilot's side so that he can see you.

■ Do not go near the tail rotor.

■ If a landing cannot be made a casualty may be lifted on the winch. Three methods are in common use: *single lift; double lift* (the casualty is assisted by the winch man); and *stretcher lift*. The casualty is placed in a Neil Robertson stretcher and lifted horizontally into the craft, assisted by the winch man. It is possible to lift other types of stretcher provided they are fitted with attachments to make a horizontal lift feasible.

There is an internationally recognised code of signals for ground to air communication. Here are just a few of the more important ones:

Δ	safe to land here
I	require a doctor
↑	proceeding in direction of arrow
X	unable to proceed
N'N	nothing found
IIIII	require assistance
L'L	all well

USE OF DOGS

Possibly the best type of dog is the Alsatian, but the other breeds have done equally well. The only restriction really is on the size of the dog (it should be big enough to negotiate deep snow) and that it has a good nose. Generally the following breeds have been successful: Collies, Alsatians, Labradors, large Terriers; Dobermans, despite their short coat, also work well. Any cross breeding from the above list should also produce suitable strains. Long haired Alsatians have not proved successful.

To make full use of the Search & Rescue Dog Service, handlers should be allowed to search the most likely areas before large parties of searchers move in. This is especially easy at night when often searches are called off, or, in bad weather when it is impracticable for ordinary search work. Dogs should also be allowed to work into the wind and if the Search Organiser bears this in mind for the dogs, speedy recovery of the missing person(s) is often possible. As a rough guide a dog is equal to approximately 20 trained searchers, but in conditions where the victim(s) may be covered by snow its potential is much greater. You should bear in mind that dogs cannot work miracles, but when used properly can be a tremendous asset to any Rescue Team. Some dogs will find bodies even when partly frozen, but dogs' reactions vary and the handlers can advise in respect to their own dog.

For search and rescue work in Britain, dogs are classified as in other countries in three groups: 'A', 'B', and 'C'. The highest standard is 'C'. The British training differs from other countries and it includes summer searches. Dogs, if required, operate at a distance from their handler to cover as large an area as possible. Abroad, dogs are specifically used for close searching avalanches, whereas here their value lies in searching snow covered areas and open moorland, where the victim can be covered with a small amount of fresh snow or hidden in heather or hollows. Dogs of 'A' grading are subdivided from 1 – 10, 'A1' being the highest standard in the group. All 'A' dogs are suitable for searching moorland and easy mountainous regions in both summer and winter. If the letter 'M' is shown on the Certificate this denotes that the handler is a mountaineer and that he and his dog are capable of use in all conditions. Certificates are valid for two years.

An annual training and grading course is held in Glencoe each December.

For further information concerning the Search and Rescue Dog Association and for a list of available dogs and handlers write to: Hamish MacInnes, Ice Axes, Glencoe, Argyll.

7 Equipment

A full list of equipment held at official Mountain Rescue Posts is listed in the Mountain Rescue Handbook. Basically it consists of a stretcher and two rucksacks containing medical supplies, though certain Posts, especially those associated with local teams, carry a great deal more.

The main items to remember are:

■ Personal clothing and equipment. Refer to the kit list on page 55 but be particularly careful to ensure that you have adequate lighting. A pocket torch or head lamp may last less than one hour so take plenty of spare batteries. Long life cells are available.

■ Stretcher. There are many different types of stretchers, the Thomas, the MacInnes, the Duff, the Neil Robertson, the Akja from Austria, the Mariner and the Norwegian Helpe to mention but a few. Many of these are designed for a specific task or for a particular type of terrain. The Thomas is the standard issue for Mountain Rescue Posts in this country though many teams are equipping themselves with the new MacInnes – a hinged stretcher constructed out of continuous alloy tube with metal runners and wheel attachment.

■ Rescue rucksacks. These contain all essential medical supplies including three ¼ grain ampoules of morphia – see instructions in the Mountain Rescue Handbook on when and how to administer and also for a list of the contents of the two sacks. They should be carried by the advance party if there is one. In the case of several search parties, each must carry sufficient material to enable it to render first aid to the injured.

■ Casualty Bag. Many posts and teams are now equipped with specially designed casualty bags incorporating sleeping bag, mattress and carrying handles. Their main advantages are that they allow minimal handling of the patient to get him into the bag, they provide a convenient method of transport to and from the stretcher and they offer excellent insulation from the ground or on the stretcher itself. Sleeping bags should be carried by teams not equipped with casualty bags (one is provided in the official kit).

■ Lightweight Tent. This is not part of the kit, but it could prove a life saver especially if the victim is suffering from exposure. On wide scale searches in bad conditions a tent with each team is a must. Some have designed a complete bivouac unit which will accommodate the whole team.

■ Search Lamps. At night each team should carry at least one search lamp capable of providing wide and narrow beam illumination continuously for at least four hours. It must be backed up by first class personal lighting and, if available, by illuminating flares.

■ Signalling devices. Very pistols, rockets, miniflares, thunderflashes and so on may be of use in favourable conditions. The agreed code is as follows: Red – help wanted here; Green – recall to base; White – message understood. Do not rely on a single flare. Release several at intervals till acknowledged. A thunderflash or other loud noise will attract attention before releasing flares.

■ Radio communications. Many teams are now equipped with portable transceivers. Most of these are on the Mountain Rescue frequency, but call signs and frequencies should be checked before departure and procedure, including time on and off the air, established. Good communications can be a tremendous asset in any search and rescue operation, but their maintenance should not so dominate the conduct of affairs that other vital considerations, such as speed and efficiency of search, are neglected.

■ Food and Drink. Adequate supplies of food and hot soup or other liquids should be carried to meet the needs of both rescuers and rescued. If the search is likely to be a long one then a stove, fuel, billies and the necessary material (tea, sugar, etc.) may ease the weight problem.

■ Specialised Equipment. Depending on the circumstances of the accident certain items of more specialised equipment may be required; climbing ropes, crash helmets, pitons, slings, karabiners and so on. In any event at least two ropes should be carried by each team since these may be required to deal with a host of unforeseen problems.

8 Evacuation of Victim

■ With the main party, proceed to the scene of the accident at a steady pace. Do not rush there as the time is being put to good use by the advance party making the patient comfortable and rendering the necessary first aid. Remember that there may be a long carry back and energy must be conserved. If there is the prospect of a very long carry make arrangements for a support party to bring food and drink.

■ On the way in examine the ground for the best evacuation route and mark if necessary.

■ The arrangement of the victim on the stretcher will depend on the nature of his injuries and the type of stretcher. Freedom from pain on the move should be the aim. Remember that a helmet may be necessary if steep ground or screes have to be crossed. Be particularly careful in the case of suspected spinal injuries and avoid any movement of the spine itself. Place the victim on the stretcher exactly as he is found – use padding as required.

■ Unconscious, exposed or seriously injured casualties are best carried in the 'head down' position with the head tilted to one side. Someone must always be in attendance in case of vomiting, cessation of breathing or other emergency.

■ A stretcher-bearing party normally consists of 16 – 20 persons working as two teams and changing shifts every 10 minutes or so depending on the terrain. A third team is useful if the carry is to be a long one.

■ If the route is not obvious and has not been previously marked someone should be sent ahead to select and mark the best line. This is, of course, particularly important at night.

9 It is the job of the Rescue Controller or of the Police to give information to the Press. If asked, give the facts as you know them, but on no account divulge any information about the victims, their names and addresses and so on. These details will be given by the Police.

10 Report to the Rescue Controller on return to base.

Appendices: Summer Certificate

Appendix A: Scheme of training

The Mountain Leadership Training Boards provide a comprehensive scheme for the training and certification of leaders and instructors in mountaineering.

The Mountain Leadership Certificate (Summer) covers basic training in the skills required to take a party on walking expeditions on mountains under normal summer conditions. It is intended as an essential requirement for teachers, youth leaders and other adults wishing to take young people on to the mountains and to show them how to enjoy their mountain walking with safety. It is not in itself a qualification for a mountaineering instructor but it does provide the first stage of training for those intending to qualify as instructors through the more advanced courses.

The Mountaineering Instructor's Certificate covers comprehensive training in all essential aspects of mountain craft, including rock climbing. It is intended as the normal basic qualification for those who wish to instruct at mountain centres or to instruct school pupils and youth groups in mountaineering. It also provides the necessary general preparation for those wishing to train for the most advanced qualification.

The Mountaineering Instructor's Advanced Certificate provides a scheme of training for instructors employed full-time at mountain centres and elsewhere. It is intended as a professional qualification for those seeking careers in this field and is awarded, after appropriate training, to those achieving a high all-round standard of professional competence in mountaineering instruction.

The Mountain Leadership Certificate (Winter) provides training in the very exacting skills required for taking parties onto the Scottish mountains under winter conditions. It is intended primarily for candidates for the Instructor's Certificates, for whom it forms an essential part of the training requirements, but it is also open to those who, having gained the Mountain Leadership Certificate (Summer), seek this particular qualification only.

All enquiries to –

The Secretary, The Scottish Mountain Leadership Training Board, S.C.P.R. Office, 4 Queensferry Street, Edinburgh, EH2 4PB (031-225 5544);

The Secretary, Mountain Leadership Training Board, C.C.P.R. Office, 26 Park Crescent, London, WIN 4AJ (01-580 6822).

Appendix B: Mountain Leadership Certificate (Summer Syllabus)

Note: The syllabuses for the English and Scottish Boards are almost identical, any differences are marked in the text: * English Board only. † Scottish Board only.

The Mountain Leadership Certificate (Summer†) will be awarded to candidates who fulfil the requirements of the Scheme to the satisfaction of the Board. *Basic Training and Assessment will be carried out only at centres approved by the Board*, as follows:

A residential course of Basic Training of at least one week's duration. A planned series of at least four approved weekend courses arranged by a Centre or Organisation may be accepted by the Board as being a Basic Training course.

A period of at least one year after Basic Training throughout which practical experience in mountaincraft is gained during weekends and holidays. In addition the candidate will obtain some practice in leading and instructing small parties of novices in terrain which is no more demanding than that suitable for Duke of Edinburgh's Award Second Series Expeditions.

Details of the year's experience will be recorded in a personal Log Book. Price £1·25, post free.

A residential Week of Assessment during which the candidate will be tested in accordance with the requirements of this Syllabus. The examination results, together with a report on the personal qualities and leadership ability of the candidate will be submitted to the Board by the Director in charge of Assessment.

Minimum age limits: for entry to a Basic Training course – 18 years; for the award of a Certificate – 20 years.

All candidates are required to be conversant with 'Mountain Leadership', price 50p (postage 10p), 'Safety on Mountains', price 18p (postage 3p), 'The Mountain Rescue Handbook', price 20p (postage 4p).

The course of basic training

Basic training will be given in the following subjects:

1 Map and Compass
2 Route Planning
3 Walking Skills
4 Personal Equipment
5 Camping Equipment
6 Campcraft and Expeditions
7 Basic Rock Climbing Skills
8 River Crossing
9 Special Mountain Problems
10 Weather
11 Accident Procedure
12 Information on Clubs and Guide Books
13 Party Leadership and Advice on Instructional Methods
14 Additional Interests.

1 Map and Compass

■ Map scales.
■ Setting of map without use of compass.
■ Measurement of distance.
■ Speed of movement on varying terrain.
■ Map references.
■ Conventional signs and topographical features.
■ Contours: description of ground from information on the map.
■ The Compass: plotting a compass course from the map.
■ Other aids to direction, e.g. stars; watch.
■ Navigation across country with map but without compass.
■ Navigation across country with compass in poor visibility (dense forest, thick cloud, darkness).
■ Location of position by back-bearing.
■ Hints on teaching method and production of simple maps and compass courses for training.*

2 Route Planning

Choice of route: preparation of route card: escape routes: bad weather alternative.

3 Walking Skills

■ Recognition of good and bad technique: attention to be directed to – placement of feet / pace / rhythm / conservation of energy / balance.
■ Procedure of party when scrambling or on rough terrain, e.g. scree, narrow ridges, steep broken slopes.

4 Personal Equipment

Knowledge of personal equipment required for mountain expeditions in *all* weather conditions. The significance of the extremes of temperature, humidity and wind should be borne in mind. Information on the principles of good design. Care of equipment.

5 Camping Equipment

■ Knowledge and understanding of the principles of packing and loading personal and communal gear. Tents and tent erection. Stoves.
■ Care of equipment.

6 Campcraft and Expeditions

■ Camp planning, i.e. Organisation and daily routine / Choice of site / Siting of tents / Hygiene / Use of mountain huts and bothies / The country code.
■ Planning of meals and cooking.

7 Basic Rock Climbing Skills

The small amount of rock climbing included in the course is not intended to train leaders as rock climbers. Its purpose is to familiarise candidates with elementary techniques, to enable them to appreciate the limits of what should be attempted by a party without rock-climbing experience, to recognise difficulties and potential dangers of terrain and to give competent help in cases of emergency. The following special points will be dealt with:
■ Ropes – types and care of (British Standards).
■ Rope handling. Knots and ties for end and middle men. Methods of belay and interchange of belay.

■ Climbing calls. Taking in and paying out active rope.
■ Skills of movement on rock – the nine basic principles.*
■ Practice of movement on rock, of rope handling, calls and all safety precautions.
■ Practice abseiling and use of safety rope.

8 River Crossing

■ Recognition of fordable and dangerous water.
■ Aids to crossing with and without line.
■ Skills and safety precautions to be practised by the individual, e.g. methods of progression, use of third leg, procedure with pack, reduction of resistance or friction, danger from trees or snags.

9 Special Mountain Problems (Refer to booklets – 'Mountain Leadership', 'Safety on Mountains', and the 'Mountain Rescue Handbook'.)

Prevention of but also treatment for –
■ The condition of exposure as defined in the 'Mountain Rescue Handbook'.
■ The chill index – with reference to effects of wind speed and temperature as well as immersion in water.
■ Demonstration and practice in mouth to mouth and mouth to nose resuscitation.*
(N.B. – First Aid requirement in Scotland.)
■ Effects of sun and heat.

10 Weather

An elementary knowledge of weather, i.e.
■ Interpretation of the weather map, recognising – areas of high pressure / air flows (e.g. Northerly airstream) / depressions and frontal systems / and the weather normally associated with these.
■ How to obtain forecasts of weather prior to going on mountain.
■ Major cloud forms and associated weather developments.

11 Accident Procedure (Refer to 'Mountain Rescue Handbook').

■ Action taken by members of the party – distress signals, first aid, routine and essential information.
■ The equipment of a mountain rescue post.

■ Simple improvisation of rescue equipment.
■ Search for and evacuation of the victim.

12 Details of Clubs, etc. Information on clubs, outdoor activity organisations providing facilities and guide books for walking parties will be given.

13 Responsibilities of Party Leader and Advice on Instructional Method – Refer to 'Safety on Mountains' and 'Mountain Leadership'.

Hints on teaching or instructional techniques will be given throughout with special emphasis on the aids to teaching. The skills of party leading should also be stressed:

■ Party leader – to choose route, set pace, appoint rear man, ensure the adequate equipping of the party and make all necessary decisions leading to the good conduct and safety of the party.
■ Responsibilities of rear man.

14 Additional Interests

Whenever time permits, lectures of background interest should cover such subjects as glaciation and flora and fauna, local history, conservation and forestry, and talks of general mountaineering interest at home and abroad.

Practical experience

to be gained between Basic Training and Assessment.

Practical experience must be gained over a minimum period of one year, during which:

1 The candidate shall obtain, prior to Assessment, a current certificate in First Aid as issued by the British Red Cross Society, the St. Andrew's Ambulance Association or the St. John Ambulance Association.

2 A record shall be kept in the Log Book of every expedition accomplished within the period. These should include not less than 16 days spent in mountainous country. At least half of this time should involve camping.

3 Every opportunity should be taken of practising the skills learned at Basic Training, i.e. map and compass work, campcraft, etc.

Further practice in rock-climbing should only be taken under expert guidance.

4 The candidate will be required to have obtained some practice in leading and instructing small parties of novices in normal country.

Note

■ Candidates will be expected to know and conform to the points listed in 'The Country Code'. (Price 6d. – H.M.S.O.)

■ Through observation of land form and of the indigenous wild life, there can be a greater appreciation of mountains. The Board recommends that on all expeditions candidates become aware of the great natural interest of the countryside.

■ Special note will be taken of expeditions which the candidate has carried out in winter conditions also any help given at a rescue or search. Where practicable, as much experience as possible should be gained under expert guidance in conditions of snow and ice but *note particularly* that this experience *is not essential* for the Summer Certificate. A high percentage of accidents occur as a result of slips on hard snow or ice and it is, therefore, important that no winter expedition be undertaken without adequate training.

Assessment

Candidates will be asked to attend, at a centre approved by the Board, a final week of assessment. Final assessment will be conducted as follows:

1 Requirements of Basic Training

The Log Book must be complete in all respects and meet the requirements specified.

2 Theoretical Papers

Pass mark 60%.

■ Mountain safety: The paper will be of one hour's duration and will consist primarily of questions on the contents of the three booklets, 'Mountain Leadership', 'Safety on Mountains', 'Mountain Rescue Handbook'. See appendix D, 1 and 3.

■ Mountain weather: A one-hour paper covering the requirements of the syllabus. See appendix D, 1 and 4.

■ Navigation: A one-hour paper on the essentials of map and compass work. Descriptions of techniques will not be required at this stage, but geographical problems may be set. See appendix D, 1 and 2.

3 Practical and Oral Examinations in all aspects of the Syllabus

4 Personal Report

The Director of the Week of Assessment will be responsible for submitting a written report on each candidate to the Board. This report will be compiled on the basis of (a) examination results, etc., and (b) with reference to a written report by the 'field assessor'. The latter must attend the three-day camp since it is there that a candidate's qualities of leadership are most likely to be revealed.

Final Assessment

The final recommendation to the Board will lie with the Director responsible during Assessment Week. Candidates must gain at least 60% in each of the theory papers. The Director should regard scores obtained by candidates as a safeguard, and in coming to his decision, should be confident that those recommended for a Certificate are competent to lead a party of novices in mountainous country within the limits set by the Scheme.

two weeks or of at least five weekends each of two days' duration;

■ Experience of rock-climbing (including experience of leading) to 'DIFFICULT' standard;

■ A current Certificate of First Aid of the British Red Cross Society, the St. Andrew's Ambulance Association or the St. John Ambulance Association;

■ Covered to the satisfaction of the Board all work outlined in the Syllabus.

Note

■ Experience elsewhere, including attendance at other training Courses will be taken into account.

■ B.M.C. and A.S.C.C. Guides will be automatically exempt from Basic Training and the year's experience.

■ Other exemptions may be made at the discretion of the Board.

■ A candidate who has obtained exemption from Basic Training and the year of experience should enter *all* his experience in the official Log Book.

Exemption

A person already experienced in the leadership of groups of young people in mountainous districts may apply to the Board for exemption from Basic Training and the year of experience. Special form available from the Secretary. To gain exemption from Basic Training and to qualify to proceed directly towards the Week of Assessment, a candidate must have:

■ At least two years' experience of travel in mountainous areas of the British Isles (those areas designated as being suitable for Duke of Edinburgh's Gold Award Expeditions);

■ Camping experience of a minimum period of

Appendix C: Select Bibliography

This bibliography has been compiled to help those who are seeking to improve their all-round mountaineering competence. Books out of print are marked 'O.P.' but may often be found second-hand or obtained from libraries. Some county libraries have themselves good mountaineering bibliographies covering world-wide activity. This is a practical guide and not intended to be comprehensive.

Mountaineering technique

(Many of these books are advanced but contain valuable introductory chapters)

Bell, J. H. B.: 'A Progress in Mountaineering', (Oliver & Boyd), O.P. – (Theory and practice with special emphasis on Scottish experience).

Blackshaw, A.: 'Mountaineering', 1966 (Penguin), 18/6d.

Burns, W. C. and others: 'A Short Manual of Mountaineering Training'. (Mountaineering Association), 3/6d.

Disley, J.: 'Tackle Climbing This Way' (Paul), 10/6d. (Also has chapters on map and compass.)

Dixon, C. M.: 'Rock Climbing' (Know the Game Series). (Educational Productions), 2/6d.

Evans, C.: 'On Climbing' (Museum Press), 30/-.

Francis, G. H.: 'Mountain Climbing' (Teach Yourself Series). (E.U.P.), 8/6d.

Kirkus, C.: 'Let's Go Climbing' (Nelson), 2/6d.

*Langmuir, E. D. G.: 'Mountain Leadership' (S.C.P.R.), 10/-.

MacInnes, H.: 'Climbing' (S.Y.H.A.), 5/-.

Murray, W. H., and *Wright, J. E. B.:* 'The Craft of Climbing' (Kaye), 15/-. (Technique.)

Peacocke, T. A. H.: 'Mountaineering' (Black), O.P.

Raeburn, H.: 'Mountaineering Art', 1920 (Unwin), O.P.

Styles, S.: 'Modern Mountaineering' (Faber), 21/-. (Recent.)

Styles, S.: 'Getting to Know Mountains' (Newnes), 12/6d.

Wright, J. E. B.: 'The Technique of Mountaineering' (Kaye), 15/-.

Young, G. W.: 'Mountain Craft' (Methuen), O.P.

Camping, walking, equipment

Balsillie and *Westwood:* 'Mid Moor and Mountain' (Boy Scouts Assocn.), 7/6d.

Cox, J.: 'Camp and Trek' (Lutterworth), 12/6d.

Cox, J.: 'The Hike Book' (Lutterworth), 12/6d.

Duke of Edinburgh's Award Scheme: 'Expedition Guide', 5/-.

Ministry of Education: 'Camping and Education' (H.M.S.O.), O.P.

Map and compass

Fenn, E.: 'Maps – How to Read and Make Them' (Brown, Son & Ferguson), 1/6d.

Gatty, H.: 'Nature is Your Guide' (Collins), 16/-.

Laborde, E. D.: 'Popular Map Reading' (C.U.P.), 8/-.

Mustard, C. A.: 'By Map and Compass' (Hugh Rees), 5/-.

Scottish Orienteering Assocn.: 'Orienteering' (Know the Game Series). (Educational Productions), 5/-.

War office: 'Military Manual of Map Reading' (H.M.S.O.), 10/-.

Ordnance Survey 1" maps are standard for mountaineering. Two useful sheets taking in popular areas are specially produced:

1 Lorn and Lochaber (Ardgour, Nevis, Grey Corries, Mamores, Glencoe, Stob Ghabhar, Cruachan), 9/6d., cloth.

2 Cairngorms, 15/-, cloth.

First aid and rescue

British Red Cross Society: 'Junior First Aid Manual' (Educational Productions), 2/6d.

Educational Productions Ltd.: 'First Aid', 2nd Edition, 1965 (St. John and St. Andrew Ambulance Associations and British Red Cross Society are publishers).

Mariner, W.: 'Mountain Rescue Techniques' (Austrian A.C.), 8/6d.

*Mountain Rescue Committee: 'Mountain Rescue and Cave Rescue', 20p. (Obtainable from S.C.P.R., Edinburgh, and Hill House, Cheadle Hulme, Stockport.)

*C.C.P.R.: 'Safety on Mountains', 18p. (Obtainable from S.C.P.R., Edinburgh and C.C.P.R., 26 Park Crescent, London, WIN 4AJ.

*These booklets are part of the syllabus of the Mountain Leadership Certificate. They may be obtainable at Training Centres.

Weather

Lester, R. M.: 'The Observer's Book of Weather' (Warne), 5/-.

Meteorological Office: 'The Weather Map' (H.M.S.O.), 12/6d.

Schöpfer, S.: 'The Young Specialist Looks at the Weather' (Burke), 7/6d.

Scorer, R. S.: 'Weather' (Phoenix House), 9/6d.

Sutton, O. G.: 'Understanding Weather' (Pelican), 3/6d.

General

Borthwick, A.: 'Always a Little Further', O.P., 1947 (E. Mackay).

Collomb, R. G.: 'A Dictionary of Mountaineering' (Blackie), 12/6d.

Clark, R. W., and Pyatt, E. C.: 'Mountaineering in Britain' (Phoenix House), O.P. (A history to the mid-fifties. Chapters on Scotland.)

Darling, F. F., and Boyd, J. M.: 'The Highlands and Islands' (Collins), 30/-. (A survey of geology, wild and human life.)

This is one of the 'New Naturalist' series;

others include 'Mountains and Moorlands', 'Mountain Flowers', 'Britain's Structure and Scenery' of interest to mountaineers. Collins' 'Field Guide to the Birds of Britain and Europe' and 'Pocket Guide to Wild Flowers'. Many of the Observer Book series are of natural interest and recently W. K. Martin: 'Concise British Flora' (Joseph), 35/-, has been published.

Fraser, C.: 'The Avalanche Enigma' (Murray), 42/-.

Murray, W. H.: 'Mountaineering in Scotland' (Dent), 25/-.

Murray, W. H.: 'Undiscovered Scotland' (Dent), O.P.

Pyatt, E. C.: 'Where to Climb in the British Isles' (Faber), 20/-.

Pyatt, E. C., and Pyatt, M. E.: 'Boys' Book of Mountains and Mountaineering' (Burke), 12/6d.

Seligman, G.: 'Snow Structures and Ski Fields', O.P.

Styles, S. (editor): 'The Mountaineer's Weekend Book'. (Seeley Service), 18/-.

Wright, J. E. B.: 'Rock Climbing in Britain'. (Kaye), 16/-.

Guide Books, Journals, Magazines

Most mountain areas in the U.K. are covered by General Guides such as those produced by the S.M.C. for the various Scottish regions. Rock Climbing Guides are also published by the climbing clubs; in the Lake District by the Fell and Rock Climbing Club, in North Wales by the Climbers' Club, in Scotland by the Scottish Mountaineering Club. Climbing clubs throughout the country produce journals which may be on sale to the public. It is always worth while joining a mountaineering club.

The British Mountaineering Council: 'Mountaineering' (3/-), appears twice a year and gives up-to-date information on every aspect of mountaineering affairs, techniques, etc.

'The Climber' is a monthly magazine suited to all tastes. (2/6d.)

'Mountain', published bi-monthly (3/9d.)

Appendix D: Sample theory papers

Appendix D1

Mountain Leadership Training Board for England and Wales: Examples of Written Questions for Final Assessment

- Outline the main principles one should adopt in clothing oneself for a mountain walk.
- Discuss points you would look for when buying a mountaineering boot.
- Explain the factors you would consider and observe when planning a mountain walk for a party of school children.
- State what effects weather and altitude can have upon mountain walkers.
- Explain what considerations the leader of a mountain walk should observe before, during and after an expedition.
- State what one should remember when scrambling and walking in mountain terrain.
- Discuss what you consider to be basic essentials of rucksack designs and manufacture.
- State the factors you would look for in choosing a camp site.
- What points would you include in a message for a mountain rescue?
- What equipment would be required for a rescue of a climber with an injured leg situated halfway up a mountain crag?
- State two conditions when morphine must not be administered to an injured person.
- How would you keep a person suffering from exposure as comfortable as possible while waiting for the rescue team?
- Give your impressions concerning solo mountaineering.
- What do you think are the usual reasons for the majority of mountain accidents?
- What are the safety factors involved in planning a mountain walk?
- Discuss the symptoms, effects and treatment of exposure.
- Describe a sequence of actions if a member of your party of 10 boys sprains an ankle on one of the Snowdon ridges.
- What considerations are involved in moving and keeping a party together on a mountain walk and scramble?
- What essential pieces of equipment would you take when leading a party of boys on a mountain walk in winter for optimum safety and comfort?
- Assuming a direct line on flat ground how many kilometres distance are there between the Mountain Rescue post in grid square 6655 and the western edge of the lake in square 6055?
- In grid square 7352 there are many conventional signs (or symbols). Enumerate them, describing very briefly what each represents (e.g. M.S. = milestone).
- Give a six-figure grid reference for your position if you can see Moel Hebog (5646) on a forward magnetic bearing of 298° and Snowdon (6054) on a forward magnetic bearing of 18°.
- Assuming a direct line, what magnetic bearing would you march on doing a journey from the mountain summit in grid square 7162 to the crossroads in 7258?
- Discuss the various factors which a group leader would need to take into account in assessing the time required for a mountain journey.
- Define a convex slope and give an example from your map. Do you consider that such slopes are good or bad routes down a mountain? Give reasons.
- What are the special problems of navigation in mist and how would you attempt to solve them?
- Plan a high level mountain walk including magnetic bearings of escape routes, from Beddgelert 591482 to Betws-Garmon 536576.

Appendix D2

Scottish Mountain Leadership Training Board Summer Certificate – Assessment: Map and Compass Theory: Written Examination – Typical Questions

1 (*3 marks*) Give a six-figure map reference for:
(*a*) The summit of Ben Macdhui..................
(*b*) The Shelter Stone................
(*c*) Glenmore Lodge ....

2 (*3 marks*) Identify the following map references:
(*a*) 994093 ....
(*b*) 045057 ....
(*c*) 927078 ....

3 (*6 marks*) How high above sea level are the following?
(*a*) Lochan Uaine 025986................
(*b*) Lochan Uaine 959980................
(*c*) Lochan Uaine 001105................

4 (*4 marks*) What is the magnetic bearing from:
(*a*) Airgiod-Meall 965067 to 950065.................
(*b*) 906046 to 911057? ....

5 (*8 marks*) Uniform Slope: Saddle: High Plateau: Convex Slope: Crag and Coire: Arete: Spur: Re-entrant.
Which of the above best describe the main topographical feature in the grid squares below?
0411 ....
9898 ....
9811 ....
0308 ....
9499 ....
9904 ....
9597 ....
9696 ....

6 (*5 marks*) How would you find North with the aid of a watch on a bright sunny day?

7 (*5 marks*) Write a few lines on magnetic variation and how it alters from place to place and year to year.

8 (*10 marks*) Describe in detail a walk along the marked footpath from 034992 to 003017.

9 (*10 marks*) You have a reasonably fit party of 14-year-olds carrying full camping kit. How long would you expect the journey to take from the Army Ski Hut 950065 to Corrour 981959 via the Lairig Ghru?..................

10 (*6 marks*) Your magnetic bearing to Derry Cairngorm 017981 is 333° and to Carn a Mhaim 998950 is 241°. Where are you? ....

11 (*20 marks*) Fill in Section A of a route card for a journey from Cairntoul 963973 to Braeriach 943999.

Total marks – 80

Appendix D3

Scottish Mountain Leadership Certificate (Summer): Mountain Safety

1 Write not more than 50 words on each of the following:
Wind chill (*4*)
Naismith's rule (*4*)
Frostbite (*4*)
Morphia (*4*)
Shivering (*4*)   (*20*)

2 (*a*) List five symptoms of exposure (*5*).
(*b*) How would you treat a case of exposure *in the field* assuming you were carrying normal camping gear? (*10*).
(*c*) What is the treatment of preference back at base and note any exceptions? (*5*).   (*20*)

3 You are in charge of a small party of 14-year-old schoolchildren who are well equipped and have already had a little mountain walking experience. The intention is a July ascent of a 3000 ft. mountain in the West Highlands.
(*a*) The mountain is unknown to you, what enquiries would you make beforehand? (*7*).
(*b*) What points concerning mountain safety and discipline would you revise immediately prior to departure? (*7*).
(*c*) What special equipment would you carry to meet your responsibilities as party leader? (*6*).
                                                        (*20*)

Total marks: 60

Appendix D4

Weather

Forecast Weather Map: Midday, Middle of February (see p. 54)

Occluded front lying across S.W. Great Britain moving N.E. at 20 knots.

Question 1
(*a*) What cloud would you expect over Glenmore at midday?
(*b*) What would be strength and direction of wind on Cairngorm Plateau at midday?
(*c*) What direction will the wind be after the front goes through the area?
(*d*) What will the weather be after the front passes and why?   (*20 marks*)

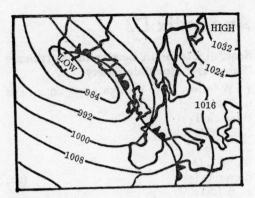

Fig. 24

Question 2

What are the air masses that affect this country in Winter and where do they originate? Draw rough sketch. *(20 marks)*

Total marks 40

Appendix D5

Expedition Planning – 'A' – No Time Limit

You may be asked to produce a plan for your own three-day expedition or, as in this example, for a hypothetical party of young people in your care.

You are planning a three-day expedition (two nights) to include en route the four 4000 ft. peaks of the Cairngorms. There are three members of the party, all have a reasonable amount of hill walking experience on Scottish Hills in summer, but have limited Rock Climbing experience. Knowledge of snow conditions is limited to that acquired by reading books and pamphlets concerned with Mountain Safety. The weather forecast is good, burns are reported to be running at normal levels, though there is a light covering of snow on high ground. High camps are planned but it is not essential that full camping kit is carried throughout the three days.

1 Plan the route giving full details of each day's journey, distances involved, estimated times to be taken, camp sites and magnetic bearings where they are likely to prove useful in cloudy conditions.

2 Give a bad weather alternative for the second and third day, should the object of the trip – the four tops – have to be abandoned at noon on the second day through gale force winds. Answers to Questions 1 and 2 can either be written out in full or tabulated.

3 Give a full list of personal equipment to be worn and carried by each individual.

4 A list of equipment to be shared between the group.

5 A list of food to be taken for the three days with approximate quantities and suggested menu. Elaborate meals are not contemplated but a certain variety is desirable.

Expedition Planning – 'B' – No Time Limit

6 Refer to your route plan for *good conditions* in Question 1. A severe thunderstorm between 8.30 a.m. and 9.30 a.m. on the third day causes burns to rise rapidly. What alteration are you likely to have to make to your route – if any?

7 You are asked to advise on the purchase of equipment for expedition use on Scottish Hills. You are assured that it will only be used between May and September. The purchaser is working to a budget and wants to get as much equipment as possible, but is conscious of the fact that it is useless to buy equipment that will not provide comfort and safety. Catalogues are supplied to assist you, though you need not restrict your choice to their contents. Suggest possible best buys of the following:

Sleeping bag

Walking boots

Rucksack

Tent – to hold three 15-year-olds.

Appendix E

Personal Equipment, including Clothing

NOTES

■ It is the Leader's responsibility to see that his party is adequately clothed and equipped.

■ See that individual loads do not exceed one-third of the body weight of the individual and in no case more than 35 lbs.

■ The delineation between LOW and HIGH level is taken to be approximately 1500 ft. above sea level.

■ Clothes not worn must be carried in the pack. A spare set of clothing must also be carried in a polythene bag and used only for night wear.

Summer

Low Level Walk	Low Level Camp	High Level Walk	High Level Camp
Map	Map	Map	Map
Day rations	Day rations	Day rations	Day rations
Boots	Rucksack	Boots	Rucksack
Stockings	Boots	Stockings	Boots
Trousers	2 Stockings	Trousers	2 Stockings
Shirt	Plimsolls	Shirt	Plimsolls
Sweater	2 Trousers	2 Sweaters	2 Trousers
Anorak	2 Shirts	Anorak	2 Shirts
*Overanorak	2 Sweaters	*Overanorak	2 Sweaters
First aid	Anorak	*Gloves	Anorak
	Overanorak	First aid	Overanorak
	First aid	Large polythene bag	Gloves
	Toilet requisites		First aid
	Sleeping bag plus inner		Toilet requisites
	K.F.S.P. mug		Sleeping bag plus inner
	Polythene bag		K.F.S.P. mug
			Polythene bag

Winter

Low Level Walk	Low Level Camp	High Level Walk	High Level Camp
Map	Map	Map	Map
Day rations	Day rations	Compass	Compass
Boots	Boots	Whistle	Whistle
Stockings	Rucksack	Day rations	Day rations
Trousers	2 Stockings	Boots	Rucksack
Underclothes	Plimsolls	2 Stockings	Boots
Shirt	2 Trousers	Trousers	2 Stockings
2 Sweaters	2 Underclothes	Overtrousers	Plimsolls
Anorak	2 Shirts	Underclothes	2 Trousers
Overanorak	2 Sweaters	Shirt	Overtrousers
*Balaclava	Anorak	2 Sweaters	2 Underclothes

(*Optional equipment depending on conditions and aim of expedition.)

Winter contd.

Low Level Walk	Low Level Camp	High Level Walk	High Level Camp
Gloves	Overanorak	Anorak	2 Shirts
*Overmitts	Balaclava	Overanorak	2/3 Sweaters
*Light scarf	Gloves	Balaclava	Anorak
First aid	*Overmitts	Gloves	Overanorak
	*Light scarf	Overmitts	Balaclava
	First aid	Light scarf	Gloves
	Toilet requisites	Ice axe	Overmitts
	2 Sleeping bags	Goggles	Light scarf
	plus inner	Crampons	Ice axe
	K.F.S.P. mug	First aid	Goggles
	Polythene bag	Large polythene bag	*Crampons
			First aid
			Toilet requisites
			2 Sleeping bags
			plus inner
			K.F.S.P. mug
			Polythene bag

Communal Equipment: Shared

Summer

Low Level Walk	Low Level Camp	High Level Walk	High Level Camp
Rucksack 1:4	*Torch 1:2	Rucksack 1:3	*Torch 1:2
Compass 1:2	Compass 1:2	Compass 1:2	Compass 1:2
Whistle 1:4	Whistle 1:4	Whistle 1:4	Whistle 1:2
	Groundsheet		Mt. tent
	Flysheet		Groundsheet
	Stove		Flysheet
	Fuel and bottles		Stove
	Billies		Fuel and bottles
	Rations		Billies
	Water bag		Rations
	Tin opener		Water bag
	Matches		Tin opener
	Brillo pads		Matches
	Toilet paper		Brillo pads
	Shovel		Toilet paper
	Tent		Shovel

*(Optional equipment depending on conditions and aim of expedition.)

Winter

Low Level Walk	Low Level Camp	High Level Walk	High Level Camp
Rucksack 1:4	Torch 1:2	Rucksack 1:3	Torch
Compass 1:2	Compass 1:2	Torch 1:4	Mt. tent
Whistle 1:4	Whistle 1:4	Thermos flask	Groundsheet
Torch 1:4	Groundsheet		Flysheet
	Flysheet		Stove
	Stove		Fuel and bottles
	Fuel and bottles		Billies
	Billies		Rations
	Rations		Water bag
	Water bag		Tin opener
	Tin opener		Matches
	Matches		Brillo pads
	Brillo pads		Toilet paper
	Toilet paper		Shovel
	Shovel		
	Tent		

Additional Equipment for Leader

Summer

Low Level Walk	Low Level Camp	High Level Walk	High Level Camp
First aid kit	First aid kit	120 ft. No. 2 nylon	120 ft. No. 2 nylon
		First aid kit	First aid kit
		Large polythene bag	Large polythene bag
		Duvet or sleeping bag	
		Emergency ration	

Winter

Low Level Walk	Low Level Camp	High Level Walk	High Level Camp
First aid kit	First aid kit	120 ft. No. 2 nylon	120 ft. No. 2 nylon
		First aid kit	First aid kit
		Red flare	Red flare
		Emergency ration	Emergency ration
		Duvet jacket or sleeping bag	Duvet jacket
		Torch	Large polythene bag
		Large polythene bag	Torch

The Winter Certificate

II The Winter Certificate Syllabus

To lead a party into the Scottish mountains in winter conditions is a serious undertaking. Demands are made on the leader which are far in excess of his normal responsibilities in summer. For this reason, only thoroughly competent all-round mountaineers with experience of winter climbing will be considered eligible to apply for assessment. Experience of winter climbing is essential because, to cite one important example, only by experience can the leader of a party learn to recognise safe or dangerous snow slopes.

No single course at any mountain centre can provide the necessary training and experience which is only acquired over a period of several years. Quite stringent requirements are, therefore, laid down in this Syllabus.

Requirements

1 Candidates who apply for Assessment must hold the Mountain Leadership Certificate (Summer).
This requirement does not apply absolutely to registered candidates for the Mountaineering Instructors' Certificate Schemes for which there are special conditions.
All candidates, however, must hold a currently valid Certificate in First-Aid as required for the Summer Certificate.
2 The scheme of training, experience and assessment will be conducted on the same lines as that instituted for the Summer Certificate.
Candidates must successfully complete the following to the satisfaction of the Board:
A. Attend a Basic Training Course lasting at least one week or four weekends at a Centre approved by the Board for the specific purpose of staging training for the Scottish Mountain Leadership Winter Certificate, e.g. Glenmore Lodge.
B. (i) Gain, after Basic Training, practical experience of winter climbing over a minimum period of three seasons, at least one of which must have been spent in the Scottish Mountains. In view of the differing snow conditions to be encountered, it is suggested that candidates should make at *least* six climbs, spaced throughout each season.
(ii) Details of this experience must be set down in the Log book price £1·25 available from the Board. Candidates will be required to present a detailed list of expeditions which must be vouched for by two suitably qualified mountaineers.
(iii) In order that the candidate may progress on the correct lines throughout his three years of experience, he should maintain contact with the Director of the Basic Training Course, and, prior to attending Assessment, he must satisfy the Director of Assessment that this contact has been maintained by e.g. attending further appropriate courses, or acting as a voluntary instructor, or by giving other evidence of the processes by which he has widened his experience.
C. Attend a residential period of Assessment, lasting at least one week, at a Centre approved by the Board. (At present, *Glenmore Lodge* is the only Centre approved to stage assessment of candidates.)

The required skills

For assessment purposes candidates will be required to be familiar with the theory and practice of the following:
■ Carrying the ice axe.
■ Kicking steps up and down in snow.
■ Use of the axe; walking, step cutting up and down, belaying, glissading, probing.
■ Braking, in self arrest technique.
■ Holding a fall on steep snow from above and from below.
■ Step cutting on ice, without and with crampons.

■ Cramponing up, down and traversing.

■ Belaying on ice – use of pitons and screws.

■ Surmounting a cornice.

■ Moving together.

■ Winter climbing up to Grade II standard.

■ Special equipment (individual and group) necessary for winter mountaineering.

■ Winter campcraft.

■ Construction of snow holes and emergency shelters.

■ Knowledge of the causes, symptoms and treatment of exposure and frostbite.

■ A knowledge of the development of weather systems in winter time.

■ A basic knowledge of the process of firnification and evaluation of avalanche risk.

■ Winter search and evacuation techniques, including the searching of avalanche tips.

■ A sound knowledge of the planning of winter expeditions and the special responsibilities of the party leader.

Exemptions

Experienced mountaineers may, if they wish, apply for exemption from part or all of Section B (outlined on page 60). Exemption from Section A and Section B will only be granted in exceptional cases and candidates so exempted will receive a modified Assessment after attending the first part of the Basic Training Course. All applications for exemption will be considered by a Sub-Committee appointed by the Board for this purpose.

Assessment

■ Candidates will be assessed on the basis of their ability to lead others in winter conditions as well as their personal competence in the various skills.

All enquiries should be addressed to: The Secretary, Scottish Mountain Leadership Training Board, 4 Queensferry Street, Edinburgh, EH2 4PB. (Tel. No.: 031-225-5544.)

12 Snow and ice climbing

The lesson plans which follow are not intended to be crammed into one or two days, but rather they should be spread out over the whole period of training. The emphasis throughout should be on basic techniques and the importance of practising braking and belaying cannot be overstressed. Braking is the one vital skill which must be taught to the members of any party going on to the hills with ice axes in winter conditions. It should be taught and practised thoroughly by all on the first suitable snow slope irrespective of their objective for that particular day. The margin of error on snow and ice is small indeed and only absolute familiarity with basic techniques will bring the personal confidence that is necessary to lead a party in complete safety.

During the period of training advantage must be taken of conditions as they arise and any programme must be flexible enough to allow for this. For example there would be little point in teaching braking in snow which was sufficiently soft and wet to make it impossible to pick up any speed. Similarly, crampon technique should be taught on firm snow and not on wet slush or 'balling' snow where they could in fact be a positive danger. If snow conditions are unsuitable for cramponing they may be just right for something else, such as instruction in belaying with 'dead men'.

Choice of terrain is an equally important factor in training and especially in the initial period when students are encouraged to 'fall off' in order to practise braking and holding techniques. A clear run out at the bottom of the practice slope where they can come to rest without harm is essential. Though the occasional rock can be padded with rucksacks and clothing, slopes with protruding rocks should be avoided, as should those which give on to steep scree. If, however, these are the only slopes available the students must be safeguarded by other methods.

This means that the rope must be introduced earlier than it otherwise would and belaying and holding techniques taught from the very first. In this way further practice may be suitably safeguarded.

The angle of the slope, too, is important. If more advanced techniques suitable for high angle snow or ice are taught on easy ground, it can give the student a completely false idea of the purpose and effectiveness of that particular skill. The ideal slope is a concave one on which a progression can easily be followed from gentle to steep ground.

Winter climbing offers great scope for the perfection of individual style. Such variations are to be encouraged and improved upon as perfectly natural expressions of a built-in 'way of moving'. There is, however, no room for slipshod rope handling and belaying or for the use of out-dated and insecure techniques. The psychological belay is seen far too often on winter climbs. No belay should be arranged that could not with confidence be put to the test. Practice is the essence of winter training; practice in falling off and braking the fall; practice in holding a fall; practice in abseiling from snow bollards and so on. It is often difficult to say that one technique is better than another especially since they may both be good, but for different snow conditions. Test and compare them in as many situations as possible. If, for example, it is belaying techniques which are being considered they should be set up and tested to destruction. In this way students will see and feel for themselves the relative merits of the different systems.

The training sessions provide the background on which a candidate for the Certificate can build his experience. They can never be more than this but they do provide a unique opportunity for concentrated learning. For this reason ascents of actual routes should be kept to a maximum of one or two, with their function more to show how the various skills learned are employed on a climb rather than to introduce and practise any new techniques. Candidates are expected to be able to lead up to Grade II when they present themselves for Assessment. The following table gives a summary of what is involved in the various grades of climb:

GRADE I: Straightforward, average angled snow gullies, generally showing no pitches under adequate snow cover. They may, however, present cornice difficulty or have dangerous outruns in the event of a fall.

GRADE II: Pitches encountered in gullies, or gullies with high-angle and difficult cornice exits. The easier buttresses which under snow present more continuous difficulty.

GRADE III: Serious climbs which should only be undertaken by parties with good experience.

GRADE IV: Routes of sustained difficulty or climbs of the highest standard which are too short to be described as Grade V.

GRADE V: Routes which give major expeditions and are only to be climbed when conditions are favourable.

Snow and ice climbing lesson plan

Indoor Session

Subject	Content	Notes
EQUIPMENT	Rope. Slings and tapes. Karabiners.	Spiral and kernmantel lay. Care of rope, slings and karabiners. Screw gate for waist line.
	Boots.	Warmth – kicking steps – taking crampons.
	Gaiters.	
	Axe.	Wood or metal – selection of quality shaft – length – design of head.

Subject	Content	Notes
	Crampons.	Fixed and adjustable – spring fit – 10 or 12 points – straps – stress great care in use.
	Dagger. Hammer-axe. Pitons. Hammer. Screws. Gloves. Clothing. Goggles.	
KNOTS	Figure of eight on the bight to karabiner on hemp waist line. Prussik knot. Clove hitch.	
BELAYS	Indirect belay to 'dead man' taking the active rope round the waist. As above using the footbrake. Indirect belay to metal shafted axe or snow stake. Snow / ice bollard. Ice pitons and screws. Rock belays.	This is the basic method.
CLIMBING CALLS	'Taking in' – 'That's me' – 'Climb when you're ready' – 'Climbing' – 'O.K.'	

Outdoor Sessions

Terrain: Slope of firm snow starting from the flat or nearly so and gradually steepening to an angle of between 30° and 45°. The flat or gently sloping run out and the slope itself must be free of protruding rocks or other obstructions.

CARRYING THE AXE	In sack. Walking up, down and across gentle terrain.	Do not use as walking stick on stony ground. Axe should be held with the pick pointing aft and the adze forward in whichever hand is the uphill one. Thus the axe is already held in the position from which it is easiest to attain a self-arrest position.
KICKING STEPS	Up gentle slope.	Position of axe – two points of contact.
	Down gentle slope.	Stress balanced position – no sitting back – axe in braking position.
	Up steep slope	Double steps in soft snow.
	Down steep slope.	Facing in using toes – axe or pick thrust into snow.
	Traversing up and down.	Use heels as much as possible – spike of axe in snow.
BRAKING	Pick brake facing slope – increase distance and speed of slide.	■ One hand on axe head, other near spike – adze close to shoulder – apply gradual pressure with body weight and chest across shaft. Or ■ Inner leg bent, axe pivoted across thigh, pressure applied on pick through forearm and heel of palm.

Subject	Content	Notes
		Other hand on spike. Whole weight of upper body brought to bear on pick.
	On back facing out. Head first facing slope. Head first facing out. Tumbling fall.	The first action in any head-down or tumbling fall is to get into a head-uphill position in which conventional self-arrest technique can be used.
STEP CUTTING	Diagonally up. Diagonally down. Straight up. Straight down.	No crampons – attention to rhythm, shape and spacing of steps – remember may have to retreat down them – always cut into the hole made by first stroke – in slab cut ∠ with pick and chop out by completing ∠ with adze.
THE ROPE	Tying on, using figure of eight on the bight, to screwgate krab on hemp waist line.	
BELAYING		See separate notes on Belaying.
	Indirect belay to 'dead man'. Practise holding second.	Active rope round waist. Wear gloves. Stress careful positioning of 'dead man' and relation to stance.
	Indirect belay using footbrake.	Practise. Concentrate on gradual increase of braking effect.
	Indirect belay to metal shafted axe or snow stake.	Clove hitch on shaft against snow surface – practise.
	Indirect belay to snow bollard.	Compare effectiveness of the different methods.
HOLDING A FALL	Second falls (without crampons).	Gradually increase length of fall up to 15 ft. or so.
	Leader falls (without crampons).	Continue practise until holding falls of up to 40 ft. – alter the angles.
CLIMBING	Grade I climb in pitches leading through.	Without crampons – use standard system of climbing calls. Stances determined by position of best belays and not by length of rope.
	Same in descent.	

Terrain: As for previous session, but with steeper section for teaching more advanced crampon techniques (e.g. front point cramponing) and abseiling. The snow must be hard.

Subject	Content	Notes
CRAMPONING	Ascending traverse.	Stress all points in – use of axe with progressive increase in angle.
	Descending traverse.	Practise with steps on steep slope.
	Straight descent.	All in 'ready' position.
FRONT POINT CRAMPONING	Up and down.	Using two axes or axe plus piton, dagger, etc.
BRAKING	Short slides with crampons.	Great care necessary.
MOVING TOGETHER	Carrying coils.	Firm rope between members.

Subject	Content	Notes
	Emergency belays – practise with one or other falling without warning.	Footbrake for emergency belaying. Apply gradual brake and ensure that axe head is pressed firmly against outside calf.
GLISSADING	Don't.	Very common cause of winter accidents – explain why.
CLIMBING	Grade I – II climb using crampons.	

Terrain: Ice bulges often found away from crag in more broken terrain. The type of ground that in summer consists of short wet walls and slabs separated by irregular terraces. More serious ice climbing should only be undertaken after experience has been gained on safer ground. In any case a high standard of ice climbing is not required for the Winter Certificate.

ICE	Note the varying quality.	This may vary from day to day according to temperature and prevailing conditions.
CRAMPONING	Up and down and traverse on easy angled ice.	With crampons.
STEP-CUTTING	As above on progressively steeper ice.	Dual purpose steps or handholds cut with pronounced lip.
BELAYING	Rock belays and pitons in rock. Ice pitons and screws.	Most effective method. Try variety of types and test to find type best suited for particular kind of ice.
	Ice bollard.	A most effective belay if fashioned correctly. Practise and test.
ABSEILING	Classic and sit-sling method from piton, 'dead man' or ice bollard. Easy diagonal abseiling.	A safety rope must be used at all times. With crampons.
CLIMBING	Grade II climb with straightforward ice pitch and cornice.	
CORNICES	Chopping through.	Second belayed well to one side – danger of wind slab on scarp face below cornice.
	Tunnelling.	Snow saw if carried makes short work of this. More advanced technique involving artificial climbing or combined tactics are not required.

13 Belaying on snow and ice

Belaying on snow is considered to be one of the most important skills which the Winter Mountain Leader must become familiar with. Un-fortunately, current literature on the subject advocates traditional techniques which are based on false premises and which do not stand up to critical examination and practical tests. For these reasons this subject receives rather fuller treatment than it otherwise would in the hope that mountaineers will be encouraged to take a more realistic view of security on snow and ice.

Ice axes were not designed with belaying in mind. Primarily they were, and are, instruments for cutting steps in snow and ice. Other functions have arisen later out of necessity, without too much regard being paid to suitability for this multipurpose role. Traditional methods of belaying place a completely unjustified reliance on the strength of the axe shaft, often without sparing a thought for the material in which it is embedded. Metal shafted axes are the only ones which can be used for this purpose with any degree of confidence, but the strongest shaft in the world is useless if the snow itself is going to fracture under the expected loading. Accident records show quite clearly that very often when a leader falls off on a winter climb he pulls the remainder of the party off with him. No doubt belaying on snow or ice can never match the security available on rock, but at the same time it could be a great deal safer than it is. In this chapter techniques are outlined and related to varying kinds of snow.

Two initial hurdles must be overcome. The first is that mountaineers tend to adopt a particular technique and use it regardless of all other factors. Many techniques are available, each one suited to particular snow conditions. The leader must be aware of these different conditions and adapt his methods accordingly.

The second point is that all these techniques demand very careful application. A badly placed axe, an inadequate stance, a rope in the wrong place, all can lead to disaster.

Types of belay. The shaded areas indicate suitable techniques for various conditions of snow

	Conventional axe belay	Indirect belay to 'dead man' with waist belay or footbrake	Indirect belay to metal shafted axe or snow stake	Bollard	Ice screws	Rock belay
Powder snow	—	■	—	—	—	■
Wet snow (porridge)	—	■	—	—	—	■
Wind consolidated snow (slab)	—	■	—	—	—	■
Old snow (soft)	—	■	—	—	—	■
Old snow (hard)	—	■	■	■	—	■
Ice	—	—	—	■	■	■

Belaying techniques must be practised

The table above shows the types of belay which are recommended for six different conditions of snow, assuming that the function of the belay is to provide some protection for the leader and the party as a whole. The degree of protection afforded by a conventional wooden-shafted axe is minimal and for this reason its use as an anchor is not recommended. There is little doubt that the most reliable belays are to be found on rock – on gully walls, on rock outcrops or even on rocks embedded in the ice. This is particularly true on ice climbs and every opportunity should be taken to secure the party to the rock, whether by piton or by using natural features. This is certainly one situation where the use of artificial aids should be encouraged. The chart must be read with this in mind. So, too, it is worth remembering that the snow cover is normally a layered structure and that, though the surface layer may be unconsolidated, there may well be a firm under-layer affording better possibilities for belaying.

Conventional Axe Belay:

This traditional method is unsafe in almost all conditions and is NOT recommended. In good, hard snow which will support the axe the leverage applied under shock loading is likely to break the shaft. Wood shafted axes in current use are not designed to stand up to this sort of strain. In snow of lesser cohesion the snow itself is the weak link; the axe pivots and pulls out.

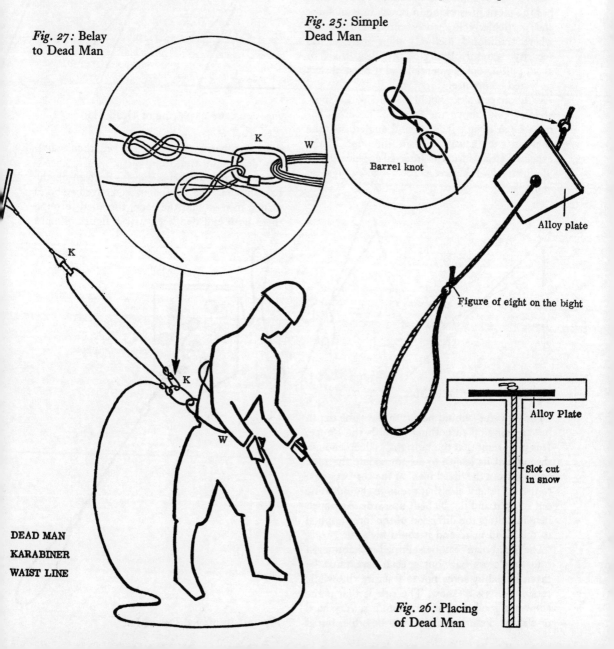

Fig. 27: Belay to Dead Man

Fig. 25: Simple Dead Man

Barrel knot

Alloy plate

Figure of eight on the bight

Alloy Plate

Slot cut in snow

DEAD MAN

KARABINER

WAIST LINE

Fig. 26: Placing of Dead Man

Indirect Belay to 'Dead Man':

A 'dead man' (Fig. 25) is an 8" square of $\frac{1}{8}$" alloy with a hole in the centre through which is threaded a 5 ft. length of No. 4 nylon rope. A knot holds one end of the rope against the square while a loop is tied on the other. This plate is then embedded in the snow in such a way that its entire surface resists movement through the snow when a load is applied to the rope. This method has the merit of working in most kinds of snow and particularly in poorly consolidated snow where traditional methods offer little or no security. Careful placing of the 'dead man' to avoid pulling out is essential and it must always be tested before use.

A 'T' shaped slot should be cut in the snow at least 5 ft. above the stance. The cross-bar must be at least 1 ft. deep and angled into the snow in such a way that the direction of the expected strain forms an internal angle with the 'dead man' of between 40° – 50°. (Figs. 26 and 27)

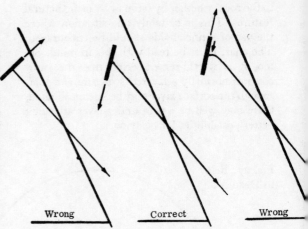

Fig. 29: Correct placing of Dead Man

it lacks cohesion, e.g. soft or wet, then stamp the 'dead man' well in.

Various improvements can be devised on the basic model. The 'dead man' can have two holes drilled in it so that the rope, threaded through them both and tied back with a figure of eight

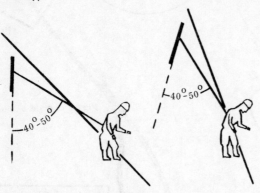

Fig. 28: Angle of Dead Man

The 'upright' should be cut to the same depth but tapering off to nothing towards the stance. It is important that the 'upright' is deep enough throughout its length to accommodate the rope coming from the 'dead man' at the correct angle to the waist, and also that the rope should come out straight and not be bent upwards. Any such bending alters the direction of the force applied to the 'dead man' and it could flick out.

The 'dead man' can be stamped or hammered into the 'cross bar' but special care must be taken in slabby snow not to fracture the whole retaining mass of snow. The rule is that if the snow has good natural cohesion, e.g. very hard or slabby, disturb it as little as possible, but if

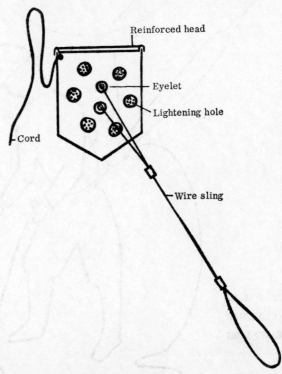

Fig. 30: Improved Dead Man

knot, distributes the load more evenly over the whole surface area. The 'dead man' must be inserted with the holes in the vertical plane (as in diagram) so that the minimum disturbance is caused to the snow. A light cord attached to one corner is useful for extracting the plate.

The ideal shape is square with a wedge-shaped cutting edge to cut into the snow and a flat top to hammer on. The top should be reinforced with a fold of hard metal to prevent deformation. Two vertical holes, fitted with heavy duty eyelets, accommodate a wire sling, talurit spliced at both ends. The great advantage of wire over rope is that it will cut easily down through the snow to adopt a 'normal' attitude to the 'dead man' irrespective of how far the latter has been hammered or stamped in. Offset 1″ diameter holes may be drilled in the 'dead man' to reduce the weight without any loss of efficiency. If a karabiner is clipped through the end loop and one of these holes the whole device can be carried over the shoulder like an ordinary rope sling.

Many winter climbs finish on flat ground on a ridge or on the edge of a plateau. It is often difficult to provide any satisfactory belay in such a situation. The 'dead man' is just as efficient buried in a horizontal position as in any other. Dig a small pit approximately 12″ – 18″ deep depending on the type of snow. Cut a vertical slot leading into the pit on the side where the stance will be taken. This slot will take the wire. The 'dead man' can then be pushed or hammered horizontally into the snow at the bottom of the pit – Fig. 31.

The climber ties on to the sling in the normal way and can then give an indirect belay round his waist. This is the preferred method of belaying. It is simple, it is almost universal in its application and it works.

Footbrake (see Fig. 32)

This method originated in New Zealand, and is almost certainly the most effective way of stopping a fall when no prearranged belay is available, e.g. when moving together. It can also be used instead of the conventional waist belay

Fig. 31: Horizontally placed Dead Man

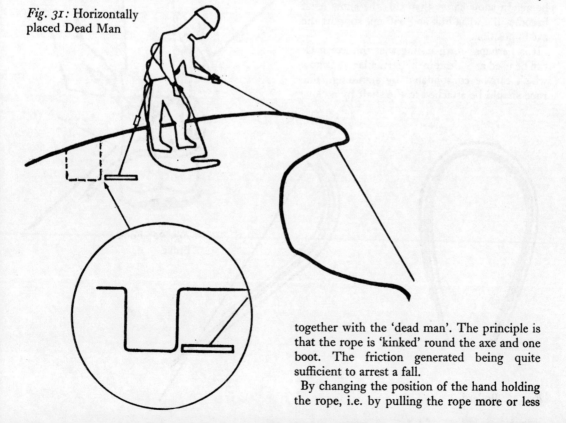

together with the 'dead man'. The principle is that the rope is 'kinked' round the axe and one boot. The friction generated being quite sufficient to arrest a fall.

By changing the position of the hand holding the rope, i.e. by pulling the rope more or less towards the ankle and the back of the boot, the amount of kink can be adjusted and thereby the braking effect applied to the falling climber. This gradual arrest is extremely important and if carried out correctly there should be no strain or sudden jerk to the belayer. As with the 'dead man' the method requires lots of practice to get the feel of it, but there is no doubt that it is effective. The main criticism is that it is a direct belay to the axe and that there is no second line of defence. However, it can be used in all kinds of consolidated snow, even with care in soft slab and, if a 'dead man' is carried, this can be put in as an added safeguard.

If the snow consistency is such that the axe is likely to lever out under load, the axe head should be braced against the side of the knee or calf. This provides the necessary stability.

Indirect Belay to the Ice Axe

The MacInnes Hiduminium shafted axe is the only one which can be recommended with any confidence and then only for indirect belaying on hard snow when the axe can be hammered home. In snow softer than this the snow itself becomes the weak link and will not support the axe in position.

It is perhaps worth noting that the axe itself can be used as a 'dead man' particularly in snow which can be consolidated by stamping. The rope should be attached to the shaft by a clove

hitch some 3″ towards the head end from the middle and the axe should then be laid horizontally in a trough cut in the snow, with the rope coming out to the surface at right angles to the axe. The whole thing must then be well stamped in and tested. The method is not so effective as the 'dead man' and can only be recommended if one is not available. However, under the conditions described it is much superior to a conventional vertical axe belay.

Indirect Belay to Snow Stake

A snow stake is an alloy tube or piece of angle alloy, 18″ to 2 ft. long. It provides an excellent belay in hard snow in just the same way as the metal shafted axe but, of course, has the advantage that it can be hammered without fear of damage. A rough guide as to the strength of the snow is to attempt to drive the axe shaft

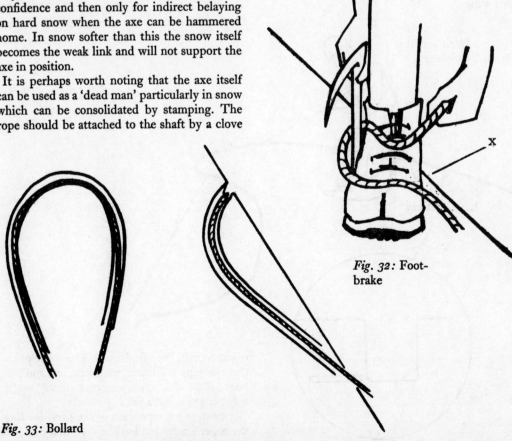

Fig. 32: Foot-brake

Fig. 33: Bollard

in a single violent thrust. If you succeed in driving it in more than 1 ft. then the snow is too soft to support either an axe or a snow stake belay.

Bollard (see Fig. 33)

This is one of the safest methods of belaying on hard snow or ice, but unfortunately a bollard takes some time to cut, especially in ice. However, at a difficult pitch or for an abseil the extra time involved may be well worth while.

The neck of the bollard should be padded to prevent cutting in and to distribute any load over as large an area as possible. The size is governed by the type of snow or ice, but generally speaking they should never be less than 15″ in diameter. Here again, it is not intended that the bollard should take the whole shock load of a fall, but that the climber should be secured to it and take the active rope round his waist in the normal way. Do not use a bollard in slabby, layered snow where the rope is liable to pull through.

Ice Screws

In general ice screws do not make satisfactory belays, not because of any defects in design or manufacture, though undoubtedly some makes are better than others, but rather because of the inherent weakness of ice. Ice on British mountains tends to be brittle and although a screw may appear to be solidly in and will certainly support a steady load, under shock load the ice may well fracture. Ice screws and pitons therefore should always be used with caution and only as a main belay when alternative methods are not practicable.

14 Snow shelters

Construction

Snow shelters, whether they be holes, caves, or igloos, can provide warm and comfortable protection against the weather. Whilst no two shelters are ever made exactly the same, their various constructions need to be based on the following general principles:

■ Roofs and walls need to be at least two feet thick, in order to provide sufficient insulation and structural strength.

■ Hot air rises, therefore sleeping shelves need to be higher than a tunnel entrance or a cold air channel must be dug.

■ Have only sufficient space between the bed level and the roof of the sleeping chamber. This ensures you are sleeping in the warm air created by your body and not underneath it.

■ The sleeping shelf should have a slight body depression in it to prevent the body slipping during the night.

■ Inner surfaces should be smooth and curved, so that water will not drip.

■ The roof of the sleeping chamber should slope from the head to the feet.

■ Drainage channels should be dug round the sleeping and cooking shelves so that condensation can drain into the cold air channel.

■ A large entrance will provide you with enough elbow room to excavate sleeping chambers. Entrance can be blocked later with either blocks of snow (if snow conditions are right), or by piling snow on ground sheets or skis.

■ Care must be taken to construct the shelter in a safe place. The site should be away from avalanche risks, not under cornices, or on dangerous snow drifts.

■ Mark the top of the shelter with a ski stick or cane, otherwise you may have unexpected company falling through the roof.

■ Fresh air is vital. Ensure adequate ventilation and clear periodically. If *drifting* is extensive the entrance should be cleared out every two hours.

In addition to these constructional recommendations, the following points should be noted:

■ A snow saw will be found to have immense

value in constructing snow shelters.

■ Digging snow is warm work, therefore strip off to avoid making clothes damp with sweat which may freeze later. (See notes on precautions in using snow shelters.)

Precautions

Certain precautions need to be taken when using snow shelters to make sure that you are comfortable inside them.

■ Only dry clothing and sleeping bags will keep you warm during the night. In addition, there is always the danger of wet clothing freezing during the night, therefore every care should be taken to see that they are kept dry and the following points need to be borne in mind:

■ All equipment must be brought inside.

■ Remove any wet clothing before settling in and place them in a rucksack. Do *not* leave this in the cold air trench, if any.

■ Place boots inside a polythene bag and take into your sleeping bag.

■ Brush off all particles of snow clinging to clothing before entering shelter. These may melt in the warm atmosphere, wetting clothing.

■ Water vapour given off during cooking may condense, wetting clothes also. If possible avoid having liquids boiling or simmering. Increase ventilation.

■ Use a torch instead of candles, or if this is not possible, use only one candle.

■ Stoves burn life-supporting oxygen. Ensure adequate ventilation at all times.

■ Insulate the body from beneath as much as possible.

■ Take a shovel or digging implement into the shelter with you.

Snow hole

■ Dig a pit approximately six feet long, two feet wide and six feet deep. Remove snow in blocks if possible and save these for sealing roof later.

■ Excavate sleeping chambers in the side walls of the pit. These need to be about two feet six inches high. The roof should be about two feet six inches below the surface. Each chamber needs to be deep enough to accommodate the

number of persons using it; for this allow two feet six inches to three feet width shelf for each person.

■ Slope the roof of the sleeping chamber and dig drainage grooves.

■ Make ventilation holes if necessary.

■ Cover roof of pit with snow blocks, etc. The last one has to be put into position from inside.

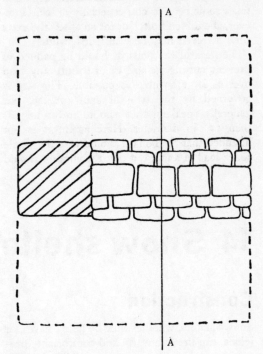

Fig. 34: Plan

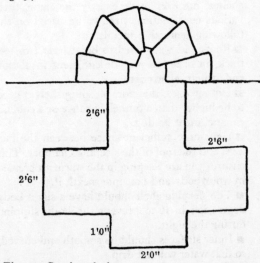

Fig. 35: Section A-A

Igloo

There are many different types of igloo, each developed in its own region and specially suited to local conditions. The type described below has been developed in Scotland and is typical of the sub-arctic igloo, designed to withstand wind and weather and above all to resist for a time sudden and sometimes disastrous increases in temperature. The thin walled variety, though quicker to construct and more elegant is quite unsuited to our conditions as it requires consistently low temperatures for construction and stability.

Any consolidated snow (damp, 'snowball' snow, old snow, etc.) can be used to build an igloo, but wind packed snow is undoubtedly the best material, cutting like a soft cheese and holding its shape like a block of masonry.

To build a two-man igloo, proceed as follows:

■ Choose a site, preferably on a gentle snow slope well away from avalanche hazard, but close to a source of good building snow.

■ Mark out an oval shape on the snow 6′ 6″ long and 4′ 6″ wide and excavate to provide a flat platform. Cut a series of steps round the bay at slope level to form a level base for the first blocks. The blocks cut in this initial operation should be saved for use later.

■ Cut a trench across the base of the snow 'quarry' using the snow saw and gradually work uphill. Rectangular blocks should be cut for the first few rows until the downhill side of the igloo is brought up to the level of the top side. Thereafter the blocks should be tapered – Fig. 37.

■ Build igloo walls with rectangular blocks till working on a single horizontal course:

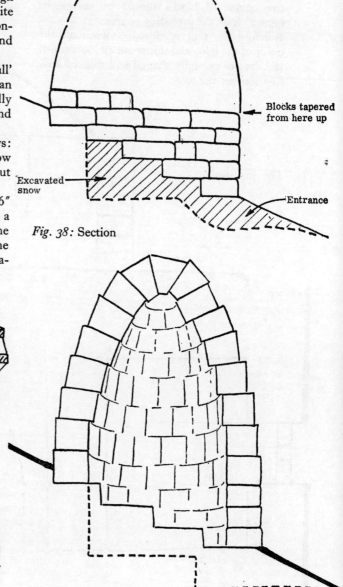

Fig. 38: Section

Fig. 36: Oblique plan

Fig. 37: Snow blocks

Fig. 39: Section

■ An entrance should be cut on the downhill side. If time permits a tunnel can be excavated under the wall and this also acts as a cold air trench.

■ Continue to build up the wall, one partner working inside the igloo and the other outside, now using gently tapered blocks. Do not try to close in the roof too quickly. A domed ridge is a far more stable structure than a perfect hemisphere – and easier to build. Each successive course of blocks should be contracted some 2″ from the preceding course.

■ Before the roof is closed, smooth off the inside of the igloo and throw out all loose snow.

■ A line of carefully shaped and tapered keystones closes the roof.

Snow cave

This type of shelter is suitable for heavy drifts of snow presenting a reasonably steep face. It is also the most reliable of all emergency snow shelters and the easiest to make.

There are many variations between the snow palace and the simple burrow that normally will have to suffice in an emergency.

■ Mark top of projected cave.

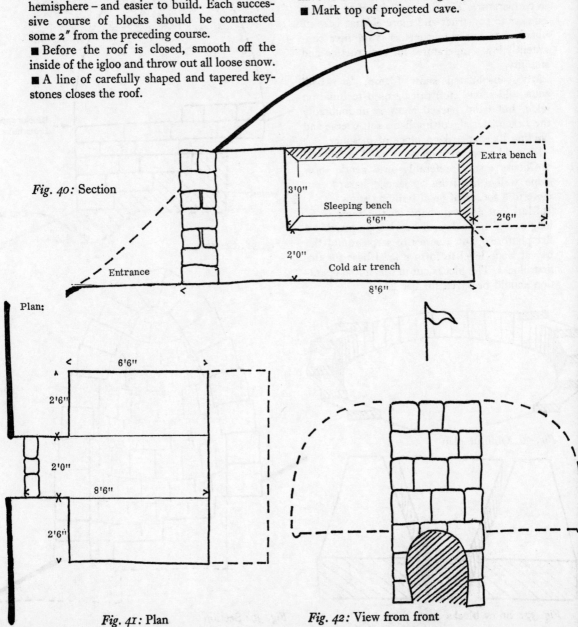

Fig. 40: Section

Fig. 41: Plan

Fig. 42: View from front

■ Dig an 8′ 6″ deep slot into the drift, 5′ high and 2′ wide.
■ Excavate sleeping benches 2′ 6″ wide on either side of the slot 2′ up from floor level.
■ Round off roof and cut drainage channels.
■ Wall in entrance completely, then cut out hole for access at floor level.

■ Make ventilation holes with axe, ski stick, etc.
  Perhaps the quickest of all snow shelters to build is the combined snow hole and igloo. The layout sketched below permits two people to dig side by side and without the disadvantage of working in a confined space. Excavation should be taken in the order 1 to 7 as indicated in the section and the blocks removed may be used later to build up the outer wall.

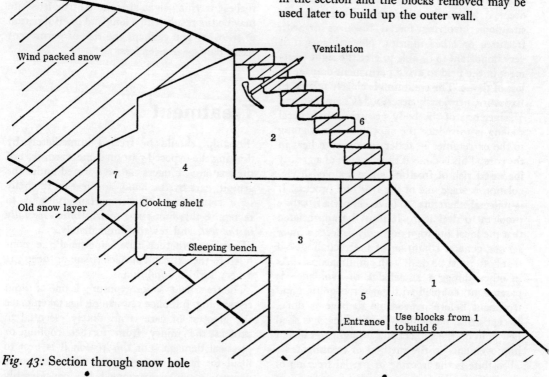

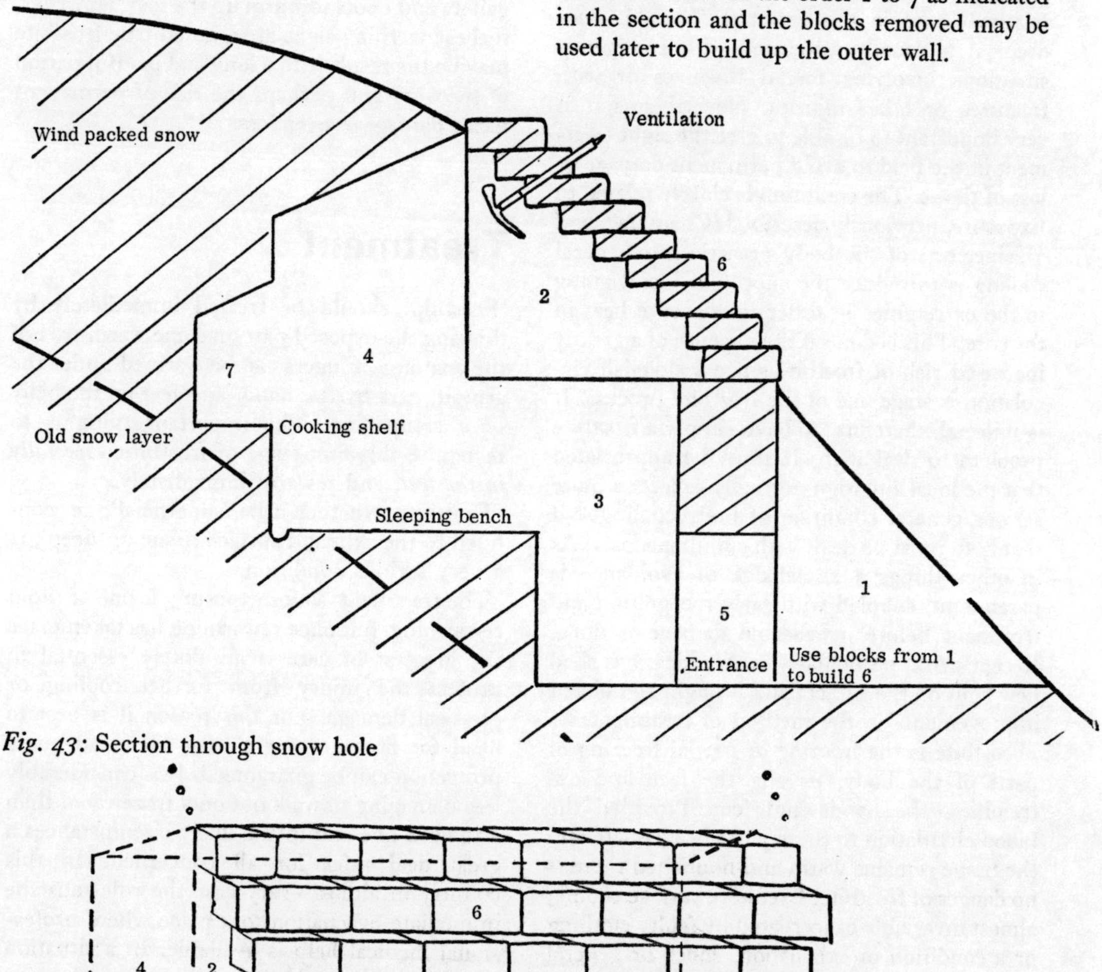

Wind packed snow

Ventilation

Old snow layer

Cooking shelf

Sleeping bench

Entrance

Use blocks from 1 to build 6

Fig. 43: Section through snow hole

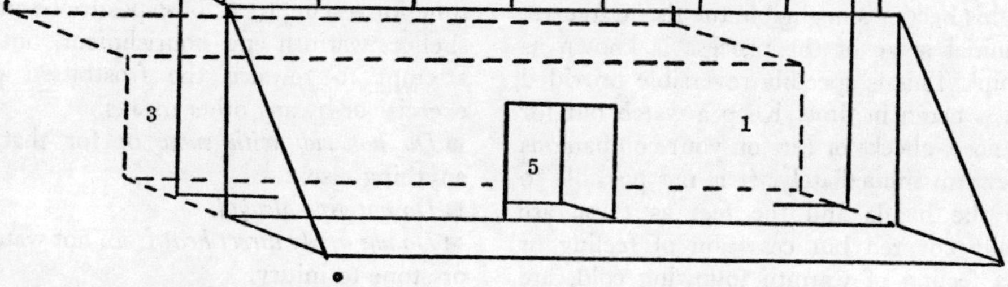

Fig. 44: View from in front

15 Frostbite

Definition

Frostbite is a condition which is fortunately relatively rare in this country. When it does occur it is usually associated with emergency situations involving forced bivouacs or with fractures or other injuries. Nevertheless it is very important to be able to give the right treatment in the field to avoid permanent damage or loss of tissue. The condition is closely related to Exposure, previously described (Chapters 6 and 7), since one of the body's reactions to general cooling is to reduce the supply of blood going to the extremities in order to conserve heat in the core. This is done at the expense of a greatly increased risk of frostbite since a sluggish circulation is stage one of the frostbite process. It is unusual, therefore, to have simply a frostbite problem to deal with. It must be appreciated that the local situation normally reflects a more serious general condition of body cooling and that both must be dealt with simultaneously. As in other things a knowledge of avoidance is paramount, coupled with early recognition and treatment before irrevocable damage is done. Recent work, particularly in America, has shed new light on the subject and brought significant improvements in the method of treatment.

Frostbite is the freezing or partial freezing of parts of the body, usually the face and extremities, the hands and feet. Provided the blood circulation to these parts is adequate and the tissue remains warm and nourished there is no danger of frostbite. Excessive surface cooling almost invariably exacerbated by faulty clothing or a condition of exhaustion, shock or general cooling of the whole body leads to a progressive reduction of circulation in the exposed part. Once this becomes negligible the tissue freezes. The initial stage of the process is known as 'frostnip'. This is speedily reversible provided action is taken in time. Keep a watch out for white nose, cheeks or ears on your companions and rewarm immediately. It is not possible to watch the hands and the feet as these are normally covered but cessation of feeling or even a feeling of warmth following cold, are danger signs which must not be ignored.

While it is fairly easy to rewarm the hands it takes a great deal of will power in a difficult situation to go to all the trouble of removing gaiters and boots to warm up the feet. However, if these warning signs are ignored true frostbite may be the result with a long and painful period of recovery and perhaps the risk of permanent tissue damage or even loss.

Treatment

'Frostnip' should be treated immediately by thawing the exposed part on some warm part of the anatomy. Fingers can be warmed under the armpit, ears by the hand, and feet on the belly of a companion. The important thing is to recognise this first stage of frostbite, *especially in the feet*, and rewarm immediately.

Frostbite, whether it be 'superficial', i.e. confined to the skin and surface tissue or 'deep', is a very serious condition.

The treatment, as for exposure, is one of rapid rewarming, but once rewarming has taken place the greatest of care is absolutely essential to protect the injury from further cooling or physical damage. For this reason it is best to head for home or for a base where adequate protection can be guaranteed. It is considerably less damaging to walk out on a frozen foot than a thawed one and in the likely circumstances a great deal safer for all concerned. In this country in almost every case the rule must be immediate evacuation to a place where professional medical help is available. In a situation where the victim is immobilised by other injuries and may have to wait some considerable time for rescue, treat for exposure by providing shelter, warmth and nourishment, but do not attempt to rewarm the frostbitten part by exercise or by any other means.

■ *Do not rub with snow* or for that matter anything else.

■ *Do not give alcohol.*

■ *Do not apply direct heat* from hot water bottle or stone to injury.

■ *Do not apply traction to fractures.*

This treatment or, more accurately, non-treatment ensures the maximum chance of recovery later. Fractures should be treated with a well padded splint and periodic checks made as to the state of the distal extremities. Shoes and boots must be removed and the foot padded gently with spare socks and sweaters and placed inside a rucksack.

It is highly unlikely that in this country it should ever be necessary to do more than is outlined above. The treatment at base would normally be supervised by a doctor or carried out in hospital. Experts on cold injury are agreed that immediate rapid rewarming for 20 minutes in a hot bath at 112°F offers the best hope of recovery and minimal loss of tissue. In the field when speedy evacuation is not possible, as on a major expedition abroad, this treatment should be administered at base camp.

Whether rewarming is induced or spontaneous, as could happen if the victim was evacuated to a warm tent at a low level or indeed if an early diagnosis of the injury had not been made, it is important to realise that further exercise or use of the frostbitten part is out of the question. In the case of a frostbitten foot the victim must be regarded as a stretcher case and evacuated accordingly. Everything must be done to prevent further damage or cooling. A dry, loose cotton wool dressing is all that is required after the injury has been gently cleaned by dabbing with warm (not hot) soapy water. Pads of wool may be required to separate the fingers or toes. A cage of some sort must then be improvised to prevent accidental damage and the pressure and drag of sleeping bag or blankets. On no account touch or prick blisters or interfere in any other way with the injury.

Prevention

Frostbite is inextricably related to the general degree of exposure of the whole body and the preventative measures previously recommended (see Chapter 6) to combat exposure are equally valid to give protection from frostbite. Basically a party that is fit, well fed, clad and watered, and in good spirits has little to fear. This assumes that the equipment and clothing worn, particularly on the hands and feet will give adequate insulation from the cold. Boots must be roomy and allow for the wearing of one or two pairs of warm socks or stockings (loop stitched). A fitting which allows socks to wrinkle up under the heel or at the toes creates local pressure points which may become the focal point of frostbite injury. Do not wear wet socks or mitts, which incidentally are much superior to gloves as far as warmth is concerned, and carry spares of both.

In cold weather keep a watch on your companions' faces for any sign of frostnip (local pallor on nose, cheeks or ears). Stop and rewarm immediately. Rewarming the feet is a time-consuming business, but impress on everyone the importance of taking action in time. A feeling of numbness or even warmth following chill are warning signs which are ignored at your peril. Remember, too, that an exposed or injured person is much more liable to frostbite and, finally, that the 'freezing power' of the environment depends on wind as well as temperature (see Wind Chill chart, Fig. 9). The effect of a 40 m.p.h. wind at 20°F is exactly the same as that of a 2 m.p.h. wind at —40°F.

16 Snow structure & avalanches

Avalanches are not peculiar to the Alpine countries. They occur with surprising frequency in Scotland. Care and judgement must be exercised at all times so that avalanche-prone slopes can be avoided. Above all, *be avalanche conscious*.

In Britain, to fall victim to an avalanche is an Act of God. In the Alps it is more commonly regarded as an act of folly. The truth, of course, lies somewhere in between, but there is a saying that most avalanche accidents are caused by their victims. To some extent at least, avalanches are predictable and though they may cause relatively few deaths in this country it is the duty of every mountain leader to acquaint himself with the fundamental causes and danger symptoms.

In recent years there has been a welcome increase in awareness among walkers and climbers of the frequency of avalanches in this country and the underlying causes of their development and release. This interest has been greatly stimulated by the publication of Colin Fraser's book 'The Avalanche Enigma' (Murray 42/-), a worthy successor to Seligman's 'Snow Structure and Ski Fields', for long the only authoritative work on this subject. It is only to be expected that the peculiarities of the British climate give rise to a peculiar type of avalanche or, more correctly, increase the frequency of a certain type of avalanche. In assessing avalanche hazard in this country, then, it is important that these factors be borne in mind, though the actual process of build-up and release remains the same the world over.

Some examples of avalanches

In the winter of 1964/65 two young men were killed and five other persons injured by avalanches in the Cairngorms area alone. Many others were involved in incidents but were able to extricate themselves without injury. On Monday, 28th December, 1964, a party of four were descending the south west slope of Ben a Bhuird when suddenly and without warning a vast slab of snow broke off above them. Channelled by a shallow gully the debris swept down and buried three of the party. The fourth, separated from the slope by the gully, escaped and was able to raise the alarm in Braemar and return with the rescue party. One body was recovered that night and the search was only abandoned when lighting failed at 4 a.m. Incredibly a second victim was brought out alive though frostbitten when the search was re-

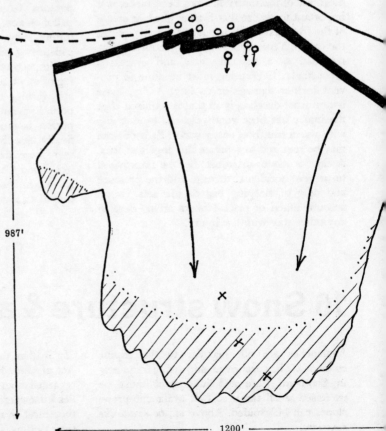

Fig. 45: Slab avalanche in Coire an Lochain

Key:

— — — Track of party

o° o Position of individuals before fracture

×ₓ × position of victims

Details:
Slab thickness 9'' - 2'0''

Mean angle of slope 28°:
Maximum angle of slope 37°

987'

1200'

sumed the next morning. The body of the fourth member was recovered later the same day

On 10th March that same winter, a slab avalanche of Alpine proportions swept away three members of a party of eight descending from Coire an Lochain to the Lurchers gully. In this case the victims were at the top of the slope (Fig. 45). The fracture line literally split the party between the third and fourth man and they escaped a fall of over 900 feet with severe bruising. Had they been lower down they would almost certainly have been killed, since an estimated 100,000 tons of snow were involved in the slide.

A 900 ft. ride on the back of an avalanche is a daunting experience, yet it pales before the 1,800 ft. involuntary descent of the Central gully of Ben Laoigh by a well known Scottish mountaineer and party. They had in fact reached the summit by the same route and were starting the descent when the whole upper slope broke away below the cornice. They were carried down and deposited shaken, but none the worse, some distance below the start of the Gully proper. Before they had time to collect their wits a second avalanche, no doubt triggered by the first, came down upon them and carried three of the party a further few hundred feet. The leader, who had moved into the lee of a large rock to retrieve his axe, was mercifully spared this second round, the bulk of the snow passing over his head onto his friends below. The total damage after this affair was a lost rucksack, which was recovered six weeks later with a camera and film it contained, intact.

Snow structure

To understand avalanches you must first understand snow; how it changes and how some factors tend towards stability and others towards instability. Assessment of avalanche risk means balancing these two. To put it at its simplest, it is a matter of attachment; attachment of individual snow crystals one to another, attachment of the whole snow cover to the ground and attachment of its constituent layers to each other.

The Attachment of Snow Crystals to Each Other

From the moment of falling, snow crystals are subject to structural changes. The most im-

portant of these leads to a simplification of crystal structure, rounding off the complex forms of new snow and producing a granular compact mass of great stability. Since the end product of this metamorphosis is 'firn' or 'old' snow the process is known as firnification.

Depending on conditions at the time of formation, new snow shows an almost infinite variety of forms based on the hexagonal system. Initially, these new crystals may form a fairly stable mass because of the interlocking of plates and dendrites, but this stability is soon lost as the crystals start to round off. The rounding-off is achieved by a process called sublimation, the change of state from solid to vapour or vice versa without passing through the liquid phase. In this case water vapour is transferred by sublimation from the points of the crystals into the valleys.

New snow may consist of more than 90% air and it is not surprising that the most effective agent in promoting firnification is a dry wind, which can penetrate even thick masses of snow. Increase of pressure and temperature accelerates the process while at low temperatures it is retarded and may in fact stop altogether below $-40°F$.

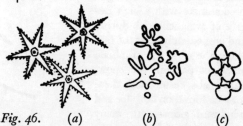

Fig. 46.   (*a*)   (*b*)   (*c*)

There are therefore three key phases in the life of the average snow crystal:

Fig. 46 (*a*) A short initial period of partial stability when the crystals are physically hooked together. This may last the duration of the fall and a few hours longer but certainly not after the first sun. On no account must this be relied upon as a safe period.

Fig. 46 (*b*) This is followed immediately by a period of acute instability varying from 1 – 3 days' to several weeks' duration, depending on conditions and exposure. The crystals, having lost cohesion, are free to move and roll independently. This is the period of the dry, loose snow avalanches so common after a heavy fall of snow in the Alps.

Fig. 46 (*c*). The snow becomes settled and as the crystals round off bonds are formed between them at their points of contact. This is the longest phase and eventually leads to the formation of firm snow. Of some importance here and particularly relevant to conditions in the United Kingdom is the continual process of melting and refreezing which builds up even larger crystals. On certain parts of the Cairngorm plateau in summer, crystals of $\frac{1}{4}''$ in diameter are not uncommon.

As with any fine grained deposit the addition of a little water to snow has the effect of increasing the cohesion of the constituent grains. Excessive amounts, however, have the opposite effect and during a thaw rain or meltwater can quickly destroy the cohesion of the snow cover. This is particularly dangerous when the thaw follows a recent heavy snowfall.

Wind has a profound effect on the attachment of snow crystals to each other. Generally speaking it accelerates the rounding off process by the abrasion of particles of snow as they are rolled along. The formation of bonds between these particles can give rise to slabs of snow of deceptively stable appearance. Where accumulation is in the lee of a ridge or peak, soft slabs predominate with a high degree of avalanche risk during and immediately after the fall. When the wind has also been active in packing the snow, hard slabs result and these may be found on both lee and windward slopes. In many cases these slabs are unsupported from below and this places an enormous load on the peripheral anchorages which may then rupture.

Attachment of Snow Cover to the Ground

This can be difficult to assess since it requires a knowledge of the hidden surface. Obviously, irregularities and obstructions in the ground surface such as boulders, trees, terracing, cross gullies, etc., tend to make for good anchorage, while fine scree, long grass and slabby, glaciated rock surfaces, etc., tend to favour the avalanche situation. Particularly bad spots are often well known locally (for example, the slabs below the cliffs of Coire an Lochain in the Cairngorms avalanche in May every year). *Find out where*

they are and avoid them. It must always be borne in mind that a heavy snowfall can nullify the holding properties of an irregular ground surface if subsequent falls have poor anchorage to the first.

All slopes of 22° and above should be regarded as suspect, though at angles above 50° it is unlikely that sufficient snow could accumulate to produce a serious slide. As well as the angle, the contours of a slope are important, particularly with regard to the line of fracture. Very often this is located along the line of maximum convexity where tensile stresses are also at their maximum. Conversely, the concave part of a slope is an area of compression and therefore one of relative stability.

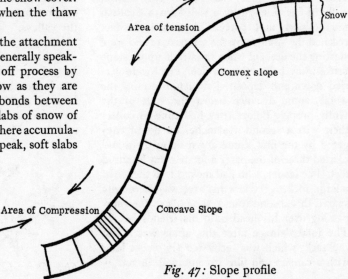

Fig. 47: Slope profile

The Attachment of the Snow Layers to Each Other

It is usually possible to cut a section through the upper snow layers and in this way examine their structure and means of attachment to each other. A knowledge of previous weather conditions and snow falls will corroborate this field evidence and suggest possible weaknesses in the strata. Crust layers, formed by the action of sun, wind or surface melting and refreezing are particularly common in this country and if the conditions are right these can provide admirable sliding surfaces for the layers above. To give but one example – it is clear that dry new snow falling at low temperature on top of a hard sun crust will have poor adhesion to the latter and that avalanche conditions can be expected. Wet new snow, on the other hand, subsequently frozen on to the same crust would have extremely good anchorage. Remember, though, that thaw conditions, so common in this country, could later destroy this anchorage and by accumulation on the crust actually lubricate the junction between the two layers.

There is another more sinister process at work which can destroy an apparently firm anchorage and indeed change the whole underlying structure of the snow. This process is known as construction metamorphism, which in simple terms means the building up of a new type of crystal within the snow cover. Fortunately, as we shall see, conditions in Britain do not favour this development, but it does play a very important part in the release of slab avalanches elsewhere.

In the U.K. the temperature of the interface between ground and air remains constant at freezing level. Between this and the normally colder surface there is a temperature and pressure gradient. Under the influence of the latter, water vapour released by sublimation moves upwards through the snow cover from warmer to colder regions. This vapour migration causes a reduction in both the substance and cohesion of the lower strata so that the whole snow cover may be undermined from within. The vapour continues its upward passage and recrystallises in the colder zone near the surface. In this way the surface layers may harden at the expense of the lower ones. During periods of severe frost this recrystallisation is accelerated and a new crystal type of extreme brittleness and size appears, known as cup crystal or *depth hoar*. A

layer of these act like ball bearings and can completely undermine an anchorage previously thought to be secure.

Clearly the diffusion of vapour depends on a steep temperature gradient, favoured by cold clear weather and also on the high permeability of recently fallen snow. These conditions are not likely to persist for sufficiently long in this country to constitute a major hazard.

The same reservations apply to the formation of a similar crystal-type on the surface. This *'Surface Hoar'*, as it is called, forms in large 'platy' crystals when the snow surface is colder than the air above it. Moisture in the air sublimes on to the cold snow surface and may build up a substantial layer of brittle crystals. Once covered by fresh falls of snow they may provide the unseen trigger for the next avalanche.

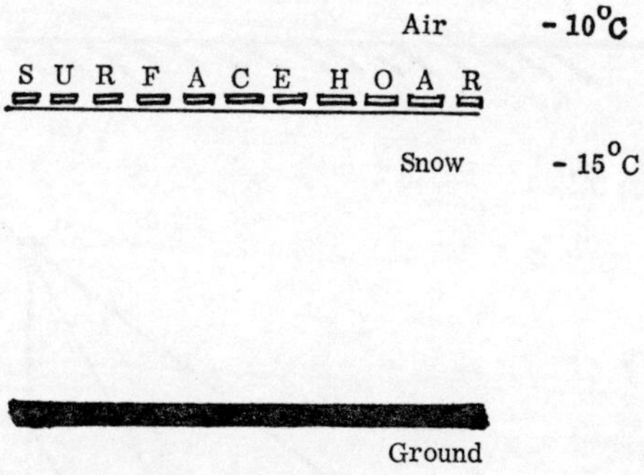

Air -10°C

S U R F A C E   H O A R

Snow -15°C

Ground

Fig. 49: Surface hoar.

In the recognition of both these crystal forms *a knowledge of previous weather conditions* backed up by an *examination of a snow section on the ground* is essential.

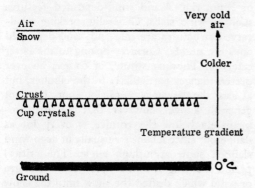

Very cold air

Air
Snow

Colder

Crust
Cup crystals

Temperature gradient

0°c

Ground

Fig. 48: Depth hoar

The release of avalanches

So far we have considered the two factors of cohesion and adhesion which together give a measure of the strength of the snow cover. Since the latter is normally an unhomogeneous mass consisting of several layers of contrasting properties, in any assessment of avalanche danger we must look for the weakest stratum where rupture is likely to take place. In such a place the strength of the snow layer or of its attachment to the neighbouring layers will be almost matched by the stress applied to it by the tendency of the snow to slide downhill. When the stress exceeds the strength rupture will take place. This fundamental concept is illustrated in the diagrams which follow:

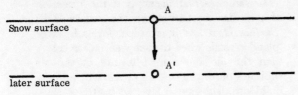

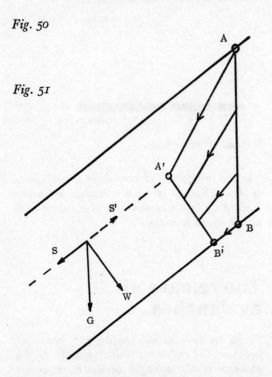

Fig. 50

Fig. 51

Where G = gravitation force; W = weight component of G; S = shear stress component of G; S' = shear strength.

The point A represents a crystal of fresh snow on a horizontal snow layer. After settling, A has taken up a new position A' vertically below A. This simple situation becomes more complicated when the snow layer is inclined at an angle.

Now the gravitation force may be represented by two forces at right angles, 'W', the weight component and 'S', the shear stress acting down the slope. This stress is resisted by 'S'', the shear strength acting in the opposite direction up the slope. This distribution of forces creates a state of tension within the snow cover which is illustrated by the movement under settling of the snow crystal A to a new position A'. At the same time, at ground level crystal B moves to B' and points between A and B to A' and B'. The resulting deformation creates tension which may be relieved by snow creep, but which may also be released by avalanching.

All this is a considerable over-simplification of the situation on a snow slope, but it does explain how the release of an avalanche may be caused by either an increase in stress, such as an extra load of snow or the passage of a party of climbers, or by a decrease in strength due, for example, to lubrication by meltwater or by constructive metamorphism.

Cornice formation

There is a fundamental difference between wind-carved snow structures such as 'sastrugi' or 'wind ridges' and wind-deposited features such as wind slabs. Generally speaking wind-carved structures are safe and wind-deposited ones are unsafe. Cornices belong to the latter category. They constitute, of course, an ever present danger particularly to the climber, but at least the danger is an obvious one. It is not generally known, however, that the scarp immediately below the cornice is every bit as dangerous since it consists usually of deep wind slabbed snow at a high angle. The critical period is during or immediately after the storm or wind which drifted the snow until the snow consolidates and again in the spring or after a

prolonged thaw when the cornice itself becomes
exceedingly dangerous.

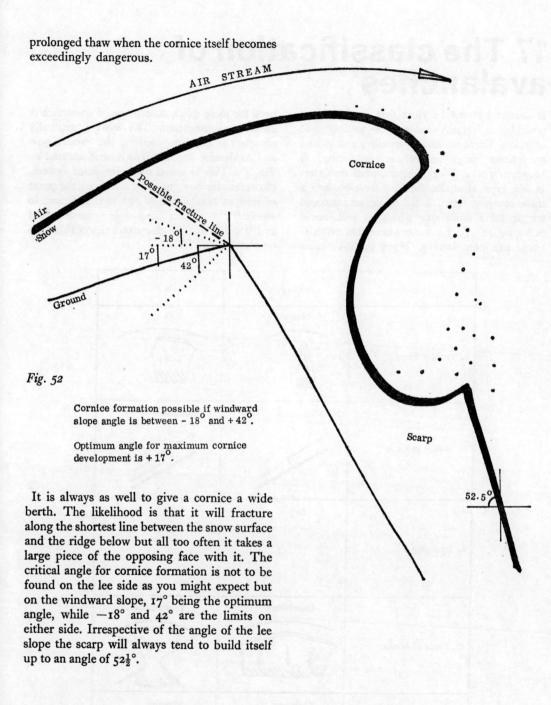

AIR STREAM

Cornice

Air
Snow

Possible fracture line

−18°

17°

42°

Ground

Scarp

52.5°

Fig. 52

Cornice formation possible if windward
slope angle is between − 18° and + 42°.

Optimum angle for maximum cornice
development is + 17°.

It is always as well to give a cornice a wide
berth. The likelihood is that it will fracture
along the shortest line between the snow surface
and the ridge below but all too often it takes a
large piece of the opposing face with it. The
critical angle for cornice formation is not to be
found on the lee side as you might expect but
on the windward slope, 17° being the optimum
angle, while −18° and 42° are the limits on
either side. Irrespective of the angle of the lee
slope the scarp will always tend to build itself
up to an angle of 52½°.

17 The classification of avalanches

It should by now be clear that it is just not possible to classify avalanches to any one criterion. There are many variations and indeed an infinite range within each variation, as between 'wet' and 'dry'. Again, what may start as one type of avalanche may develop into a more complex form. A fall of ice seracs could trigger off a wind slab which in turn could pulverise into a dry powder avalanche, part airborne and part flowing. There is, however, a need for some quick descriptive, if scientifically inexact, classification. The system generally accepted is that proposed by the Swiss Snow and Avalanche Research Institute illustrated by Fig. 53. This is based on a five-point system. However, for our purposes and from the point of view of recognition of risk it is sufficient to consider three main types only: Powder, Wet and Wind Slab. The characteristics of these are tabulated below:

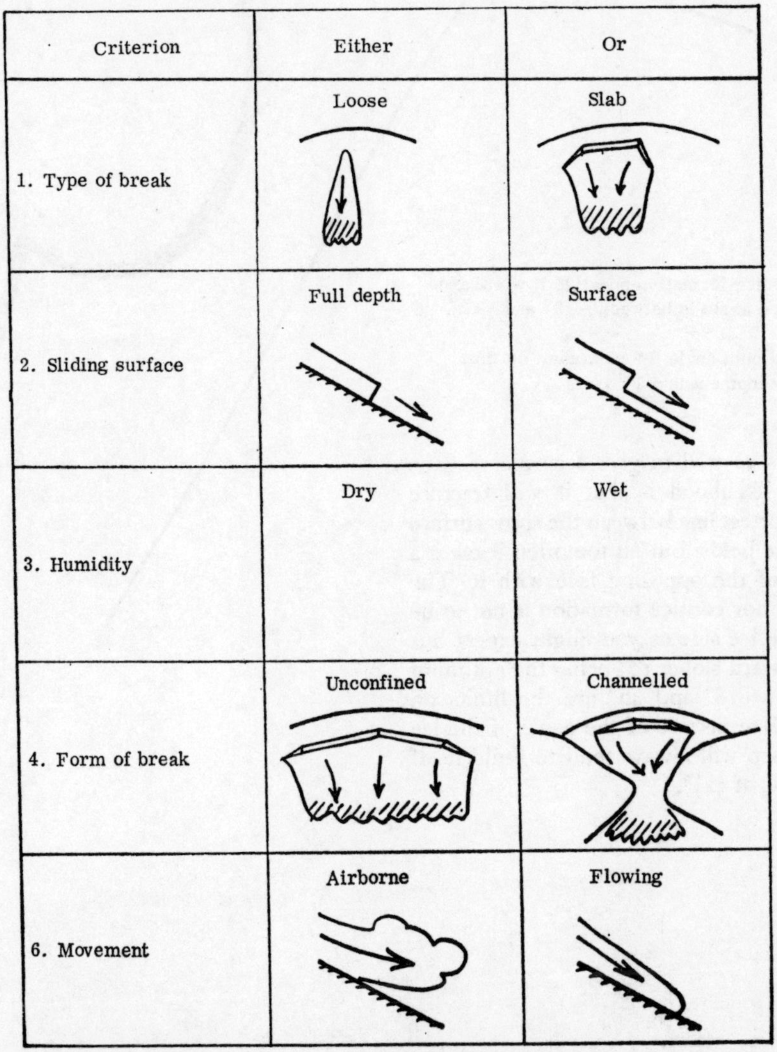

Criterion	Either	Or
1. Type of break	Loose	Slab
2. Sliding surface	Full depth	Surface
3. Humidity	Dry	Wet
4. Form of break	Unconfined	Channelled
6. Movement	Airborne	Flowing

Fig. 53

Powder

Occurrence	Characteristics	Danger Signs
1 Dominant Winter type in cold, dry conditions. Not common in U.K.	1 Starts silently as loose snow avalanche, i.e. it starts from a single point and not as a slab.	1 Any fall of dry new snow in excess of 9″, or area of thick local accumulation.
2 On slopes of 22° or more, the higher the altitude the greater and more prolonged the risk.	2 May be flowing, airborne or a combination of the two. The airborne form is the more devastating.	2 Where dry new snow falls on crust, be it caused by wind, sun or frozen wet snow.
3 North and East facing slopes may remain avalanche prone for weeks till settled.	3 Many achieve great speed and turbulence.	3 A sudden rise in temperature after a fall.
4 South facing slopes will settle after two or three days of fine weather.	4 Preceded and accompanied by a powerful blast.	4 Sunballs. Snowballs trickling down a slope under the melting action of the sun on the surface layer.

Wet

1 Dominant Spring type. Larger ones follow well defined tracks.	1 Loose or slab in form, with characteristic 'ruffled carpet' start.	1 Sudden rise in temperature especially in humid and over-cast conditions and following heavy fall of snow.
2 Fall on relatively shallow gradients at all altitudes in thaw conditions.	2 Flowing and develops roar similar to a waterfall. Contains snow boulders.	2 Wet snowfalls, rain and warm wet winds.
3 Early afternoon critical time in fair weather.	3 Moves relatively slowly and can therefore sometimes be outrun by a competent skier.	3 Sticky snow. Large snowballs penetrating deep into cover.
4 May start below rocks which cause local thawing.	4 Debris consolidates under great pressure and freezes instantly.	4 Cracks and rifts in the snow cover.
		5 Slopes scarred by previous avalanches.

Wind slab

1 Throughout the Winter wherever wind blown snow has accumulated. The scarp below a cornice is a particularly dangerous area.	1 Slab, normally surface and flowing.	1 Wind slab has a chalky, non-reflective appearance and may have a deceptively firm surface. Harmless slabs on safe ground may settle suddenly underfoot or break off into small straight-edged pieces.
2 Soft slabs form normally on the lee slopes of peaks and ridges during or immediately after a storm.	2 Starts with or without a loud report, the entire slab breaking into a mass of smaller pieces.	2 A slab may become buried beneath layers of apparently safe snow.

3 'Hard slab' is the most dangerous type of avalanche, because its firm surface encourages a false sense of security. May remain dangerous for several weeks.

3 May pulverise to the form of a dry powder avalanche.

3 Due to contraction of the layers below an air space may be created.

4 'Soft slabs' often released during heavy snow falls when wind of 10 – 20 m.p.h. or over.

4 Debris remains as blocks – hard slab. Debris similar to powder avalanche – soft slab.

4 Wind ripples or waves indicate that slabs may be found nearby.

In conclusion let us look at our winter weather pattern and see how it affects the frequency and type of avalanche to be expected in this country.

In the first place we have a relatively low snow fall; this means that avalanches are considerably less frequent and less widespread in their occurrence. Add to this the shorter slope length and the fact that falls in excess of two feet are exceedingly rare and you have a situation which precludes the possibility of devastating slides on an Alpine scale.

Nevertheless there are factors which operate against the foregoing and the most important of these is wind. The snow cover may be slight but the ubiquitous wind redistributes it into the gullies and on to the lee slope where it can accumulate to enormous depths in thick snow cushions or in the sinister garb of wind slab. However, the field is narrowed thereby and these places can be avoided. If the last heavy snowfall came on a south west wind then keep clear of all north east facing slopes until conditions have stabilised. In particular, beware of soft slab avalanches in these areas during or immediately after a storm and hard slab avalanches over a longer period, especially when conditions remain cold.

Rapid changes in the weather pattern are characteristic of the United Kingdom, with relatively high average winter temperatures with the freezing level bobbing up and down our mountain sides with astonishing rapidity. This not only hinders the accumulation of snow but also tends to have a settling effect in that it favours the process of firnification. At the same time it encourages the development of crust layers. These crusts may be produced by wind or sun or by melting and refreezing. But whatever the cause, they are a potential source of danger when covered by further snow falls. Wind transported snow, or dry new snow, falling on such crusts gives rise to avalanche conditions.

Rain can fall at any time throughout the winter. It has little effect on spring snow, but it can give rise to dangerous conditions earlier in the year where heavy slabs of snow are poorly anchored to the underlayer. A feature of our winter is the protracted spring when well consolidated sugary snow lingers on the tops and in the gullies. Wet snow avalanches are uncommon since by this time the snow is well consolidated and later falls are shallow and rarely subjected to the drastic thaws of the Alpine spring. The risk at this time of year is not so much from wet snow as from old snow whose attachment to the ground has been undermined by percolating water. The paths of these spring avalanches are often well known locally where some peculiarity of the ground favours their release. For instance the avalanche of old snow in Coire an Lochain in the Cairngorms takes place every year in early May or thereabouts and is caused by the action of water in breaking the bond between the great snow mass (up to 25 feet thick) and the 600 feet sheet of smooth granite slabs below.

18 Avalanche search and rescue

Speed is of paramount importance in any avalanche operation. The chances of survival are greatly reduced as the burial time increases.

Few victims are brought out alive after two hours or more in the snow. The operation may be considered in three phases:

■ a preliminary search by the survivors of the avalanche;

■ an advance party search carried out with the men and equipment that can be got to the site without delay;

■ a systematic search using probes, dogs and other methods of detection.

Search by survivors

It is of vital importance that the position of the victims when engulfed and when last seen be marked on the ground. The line connecting these two points acts as a pointer to the likely burial area. This area and indeed the whole of the debris should be examined as closely as time permits for any sign of the victim, his clothing or equipment. A reversed ski stick or

a stick with the basket removed makes a simple probe to test likely spots.

Obviously the amount of time devoted to this preliminary search depends on the location of the accident and the number of survivors. However, this surface search is absolutely essential and half an hour to an hour is suggested as being of the right order.

Advance party search

An advance party must be sent immediately and with all speed to the site of the avalanche. They should take with them only what is immediately available in the form of first aid, shovels and sounding rods or sticks. It is the job of this party to follow up the preliminary search and concentrate their attention on the most likely area of debris.

Systematic search

A great many people may be involved in this phase and a high degree of accuracy and co-ordination is essential. For these reasons the search must be conducted with military precision and must be under the direct control of one man.

In spite of all the scientific advances in this field the two oldest methods of search remain the most effective, namely the use of sounding rods or probes and the use of dogs.

Use of Sounding Rods

These come in a variety of forms but are normally jointed metal rods up to 12 ft. in length. The rescuers are arranged in an extended line across the debris and advance up the slope probing at set intervals and to a set depth. An area once searched in this way should be clearly marked with flags or sticks.

It is normal to probe to a depth of 6 ft. even although the depth of the debris may be considerably greater. The saving in time far outweighs the slim chance of finding a victim alive at a greater depth. Even with a team of 20–30 people the business of probing takes a very long time and here again a saving can be made by adopting a wide spacing between probes. Rescuers stand with their feet 2 ft. apart and

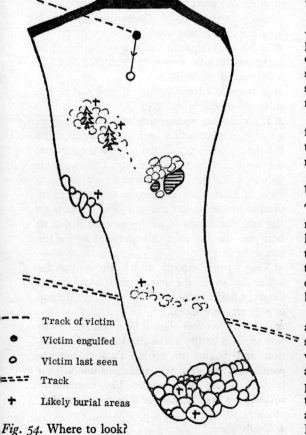

- - - Track of victim

● Victim engulfed

○ Victim last seen

=--= Track

✝ Likely burial areas

Fig. 54. Where to look?

separated from their neighbours' feet by a distance of 1 ft.

For coarse probing the rods are driven in between the feet. The whole line then advances by one 3 ft. pace and the process is repeated. In this way a 3 ft. square grid is built up.

For fine probing the rods are driven in at both toes and also centrally. The line then advances by 1 ft. and the process is repeated. In this way a 1 ft. grid is built up.

The great disadvantage of sounding, effective though it is, is the length of time it takes to cover the ground, even with large numbers of rescuers. It is for this reason that a well trained dog is worth its weight in gold for it can search a given area in a tenth of the time that it would take a team of 20 men.

Use of Avalanche Trained Dogs

Details of the Search and Rescue Dog Association have been given on page 42.

If dogs are to be used at all they should be brought to the site of the accident as soon as possible. There is no reason why the search should be delayed till their arrival, provided the area is cleared 10–15 minutes before they are set to work. The rescuers must of course move off down-wind of the area.

Trenching

If these methods fail to locate the victim trenches must be dug into the debris. These trenches should be approximately 1 yard wide and spaced at intervals of 3 yards. The walls of the trenches should then be probed horizontally.

Other Methods

Many other ingenious methods of detection have been devised. They can be divided roughly into those which require the victim to carry some device such as a VHF transmitter or a magnetic disc (Foster sonde and Varian) and those which depend on some natural function or property of the body. The latter offer the best hope for development since it is always difficult to persuade people to carry extra equipment, no matter how compact.

What to do if caught in an avalanche

This is the sort of advice which is easy to give but which may be quite impossible to follow. However, it is the distillation of the experience of many victims over a period of years. There are of course a number of physical variables, to say nothing of human ones, and the best course of action depends to a large extent on them. For instance, what may be a number one priority in a powder snow avalanche may be of little importance in a slab one.

■ Remove rucksack and skis (these should already be in the quick release position if there is any risk of avalanche). A good skier may of course be able to schuss out of danger.

■ Make a quick assessment of the avalanche; whether you are at the top, bottom, middle, or to one side; what type it is (wet, dry, etc.) and where your best line of release lies. There may be a handy crevasse nearby!

■ Delay your departure as long as possible. The more you let past you at the start the less will bury you at the finish.

■ It may be advantageous to work out to the side of the avalanche.

■ If swimming movements are possible, then a sort of double-action back stroke seems to be the most effective, with the back to the force of the avalanche and the head up. Obviously, if you are in danger of being struck by blocks and slabs of snow then your arms will have to be used to protect your head and face. There is no cut and dried procedure here – ride it out as best you can and save your great effort for the last seconds.

■ Keep your mouth shut! In a powder avalanche cover the mouth and nose with a handkerchief or other piece of clothing (the top of a sweater or anorak).

■ A supreme effort should be made in the last few seconds as the avalanche loses its momentum and begins to settle. Two things are paramount: an air space; and a position as near to the surface as possible. The chances of survival are greatly reduced if buried deep (4 ft. plus).

■ Don't panic!

When crossing suspected avalanche slope

remember to . . .

■ Loosen your ski bindings and safety straps and to take your hands out of stick straps.

■ Loosen rucksack straps and be prepared to shed any other impediments.

■ Secure your anorak hood over your mouth and nose if possible.

■ Trail an avalanche cord. This is a 50 ft. length of brightly coloured nylon tied to the waist at one end and left to trail behind you on the snow. Should you be taken by an avalanche it is likely that some part of this light cord will be thrown up on the surface, even if you are not. The cord has metal tags crimped on at 2 metre intervals with an arrow and the number of metres to the end of the cord (in the direction of the arrow) marked on. Just make sure you tie on to the right end of the cord!

■ Go down on foot rather than ski.

■ Go straight down rather than make a descending traverse.

■ Cross high and if possible on a concave slope. The latter is generally more stable than other slopes and the higher you are the less chance there is of being buried.

■ Cross one at a time. Never assume that the passage of another party is proof that the slope is safe. They may well be the first pressure on the trigger.

BOOKS TO READ

Department of Agriculture Handbook No. 194. 'Snow Avalanches', U.S. Government Printing Office.

'Snow Structure and Ski Fields', by Seligman.

'Avalanche Enigma', by Colin Fraser (Murray, 42/-).

'Handbook of Ski Mountaineering', by D. R. Brower, Sierra Club, San Francisco.

'Mountaineering – The Freedom of the Hills', by Mountaineers Incorporated.

'Snow and its Metamorphosis', by Snow, Ice and Permafrost Research Establishment, translation No. 14. U.S. Army Corps of Engineers.

'The ABC of Avalanche Safety' – A. Chapelle (Editor), Highlander Publishing Co., Boulder, Colorado.

'Ski Touring and Glacier Ski-ing', Ski Club of Great Britain, 118 Eaton Square, London, S.W.1.

FILMS TO SEE

'Dial Double One', Petroleum Films Bureau, 4 Brook Street, London, W.1.

'Avalanche Control', Regional Office, Forest Service, U.S. Department of Agriculture.

© *The Scottish Council of Physical Recreation 1969. Printed by Eyre and Spottiswoode Limited at The Thanet Press, Union Crescent, Margate*